STUDIES IN THE UK ECONOMY

Green economics

David Burningham
Brunel University

and

John Davies
Coleg Harlech, Gwynedd

Series Editor
Bryan Hurl
Head of Economics, Harrow School

Heinemann Educational Publishers
Halley Court, Jordan Hill, Oxford OX2 8EJ
a division of Reed Educational & Professional Publishing Ltd

MELBOURNE   AUCKLAND

FLORENCE   PRAGUE   MADRID   ATHENS

SINGAPORE   TOKYO   SAO PAULO

CHICAGO   PORTSMOUTH (NH)   MEXICO

IBADAN   GABORONE   JOHANNESBURG

KAMPALA   NAIROBI

British Library Cataloguing in Publication Data
A catalogue record for this book is available from the British Library

ISBN 0 435 33025 X

Typeset and illustrated by TechType, Abingdon, Oxon.
Printed and bound in Great Britain by Clays Ltd, St Ives plc

Acknowledgements

The publishers would like to thank the following for permission to reproduce copyright material:

Associated Examining Board for the questions on pp. 33, 43, 54, 65–7, 86; the Commission of the European Communities for the extract on p. 84; © *The Economist*, London, for the extracts on pp. 9, 76, 86–7; *Financial Times* for the extracts on pp. 11, 23, 34, 44–5, 51, 65–6, 78; *The Guardian* for the extract on p. 70; Her Majesty's Stationery Office for the extracts from *This Common Inheritance*, first report, 1990, second report, 1992 and third report, 1994, on pp. 77, 79, 80, 82, and for the extract from the Department of Transport's *Design Manual for Roads and Bridges*, volume II, on p. 84, Crown copyright is reproduced with the permission of the Controller of HMSO; Newspaper Publishing plc for the extracts from *The Independent* on pp. 73, 74; Northern Examinations and Assessment Board for the questions on pp. 24, 33, 43, 65, 75; Oxford and Cambridge Schools Examination Board for the questions on pp. 11, 25, 65; Prentice Hall for the diagram on p. 55, taken from *Economics Workbook* by J. Sloman and M. Sutcliffe, 1991; the Punch Library for the cartoon by Noel Ford on p. 4 and the cartoons by Norman Thelwell on pp. 39, 48; Bryan Reading for the cartoon on p. 17, published and reproduced by permission of *The Oldie*; University of Cambridge Local Examinations Syndicate for the questions on pp. 10, 24, 44, 54–6, 86; University of London Examinations and Assessment Council for the questions on pp. 11–12, 24, 34, 44–5, 75, 76, 86–7; University of Oxford Delegacy of Local Examinations for the question on p. 33; Welsh Joint Education Committee for the question on pp. 10–11; Welsh Water plc for the information on p. 15; *Yorkshire Evening Post* for the adapted article on p. 25.

The publishers have made every effort to contact the correct copyright holders. However, if any material has been incorrectly acknowledged, the publishers would be happy to make the necessary arrangements at the earliest opportunity.

Contents

Preface

Green economics has moved up to the front rank in the new SCAA-approved syllabuses. You can find no better confirmation of this than in a leading examinations board's current Objective Test booklet – there the first six questions include three that are dealt with in this book. One of the questions reads:

Production activity as part of an environmental closed cycle implies:
(a) government activity to internalize the social costs of pollution
(b) an economic model of resource allocation without a public sector
(c) an economic model of resource allocation that ignores foreign trade
(d) the recycling of material as an input into the productive process.

Publication of the Pearce Report, *Blueprint for a Green Economy*, turned what was a minor part of the syllabus into a fashionable topic. It has also spawned an awareness in the young of the commercial response of opportunist firms and some pragmatic governments.

Green economics is now accepted as an integral part of current study, so it qualifies as an essential addition to the series *Studies in the UK Economy*.

Bryan Hurl
Series Editor

Introduction

'People everywhere are offended by pollution. They sense intuitively
that we have pressed on limits we should have not exceeded. They
want to clean up the World, make it a better place, be good trustees of
the Earth for future generations.'
James Speth, President of the World Resource Institute

This book is about the contribution economics can make to the solution of environmental problems. We intend to show that, although the challenges referred to by James Speth in the quotation above are tasks for, among others, scientists and conservationists, they also raise questions about choice and efficiency in the use of limited resources. They are therefore part of the study of economics.

- **Chapter 1** reviews the questions economists ask about the environment.

- **Chapter 2** examines the economic causes of environmental problems.

- **Chapter 3** continues with those themes and discusses what is meant by 'efficient' pollution.

- **Chapter 4** explores the relationships between growth and environmental damage.

- **Chapter 5** looks at the question of how we decide upon the amount of resources needed to save and improve the environment.

- **Chapters 6, 7 and 8** discuss the measures that can be taken to improve the management of environmental resources, from both theoretical and practical standpoints, with reference to UK and European experience.

Chapter One

The environment and the economy

'I shot an arrow in the air. It stuck!'
Tom Lehrer, songwriter and mathematician

Preliminaries

The plight of the world environment may provoke solemn statements, or wry jokes of the kind quoted above. Whatever our response, the environment is clearly a matter of widespread anxiety and fascination guaranteed a prominent place in television and newspaper headlines. Major disasters in the 1980s, such as:

- the massive radiation leak from the Ukrainian nuclear plant at Chernobyl
- the Alaskan oil spill from the Esso tanker Valdez, and
- the devastating explosion, killing 6600 people, at a chemical plant in Bophal, India

have helped to focus attention on the serious environmental impact of human activities.

In the United Kingdom the efforts of **Greenpeace, Friends of the Earth** and the **Green party** have ensured that the environment is firmly on the political agenda. The publication in 1990 of *This Common Inheritance* – the first official survey of all aspects of the UK environment – signalled the government's involvement. Today all political parties claim to be 'green', as do most large corporations.

Since one country's pollution can be every country's problem, let us look for a moment at the environment from a global perspective. According to a recent, much publicised, United Nations report, glaciers are shrinking, sea levels rising and the planet is warming (Figure 1).

The gloomy statistics of this report also portray a world in which natural stocks and resources are dwindling as demand increases. If the trends continue, it is claimed that dependable supplies of ocean and freshwater fish, and of fertile land, may be depleted within two generations.

How seriously should we regard these forecasts and what have they to do with economics? This book explores two questions:

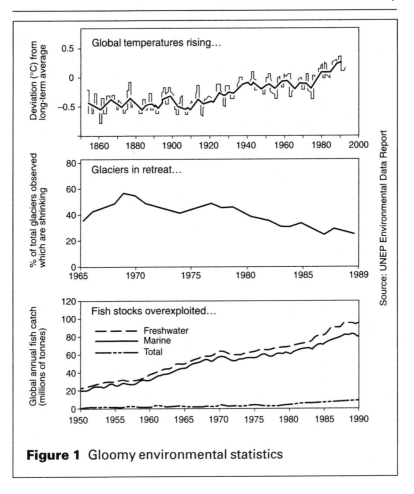

Figure 1 Gloomy environmental statistics

- To what extent are environmental problems also economic problems?
- From our toolkit of economic ideas and techniques, are there any that we can use to help us repair or check the damage to our planet?

Before tackling these questions we need to be clear about the nature of the major threats to the earth's environment. These have been a source of considerable confusion in the public mind, for several reasons:

- *Eco-systems* – the relationships between living things and their surroundings – are very complex. Scientists are not yet in agreement about the significance of some of the environmental threats or ways in which they occur.

- The complicated physics and chemistry of climate are also equally difficult for scientists to understand. Good and bad effects may coexist. Recent research, for example, has shown that sulphur dioxide gas, released when coal and oil are burnt, creates a protective haze that reflects some sunlight back into space, thereby slowing the harmful global warming effect arising from human activities. Unfortunately for us, sulphur dioxide also contributes to acid rain, damaging lakes and forests.

- Further confusion can arise in the mind of the keen citizen with an interest in the environment, because some desirable green activities may have undesirable side-effects. The loyal, green car owner, having fitted a catalytic converter to reduce exhaust emissions, may be dismayed to hear experts pronounce that the benefits are offset by higher fuel consumption. Some green pressure groups themselves are partly responsible for confusion over the extent of environmental damage. In an effort to promote their cause, they may offer a doomsday scenario which plays down progress in managing the environment – the reduction in the use of harmful chemicals such as CFCs, for example.

- Doom-laden forecasts, if proved wrong, may misfire, by reducing interest in things that should be matters of serious concern. In 1968, two influential studies, *Limits of Growth and Mankind at the Turning Point*, predicted, on the basis of a computer model of the world, widespread catastrophe and international collapse of economies within two decades, as natural resources were exhausted. The world demand for petroleum was forecast to exceed

"But you had £5 only last week."

supply by 1990. *The computer model failed to incorporate the elementary economic lesson that scarcity drives up prices and prompts a search for new reserves and alternatives.* Nevertheless, over twenty years later, population growth – the basis of these forecasts – is still a real and persistent problem.

- Fashion and sentimentality also add to our misunderstanding about environmental problems. Politicians, media stars and various pressure groups gain useful publicity by their visible support of popular 'green' concerns. Public attention and funds are then focused on the necessity of saving spectacular whales or cuddly giant pandas. The disappearance of less attractive species, such as the Central American Harlequin Beetle or Brazilian Pit Viper – whose venom is useful to our understanding of the treatment of high blood pressure – go unnoticed.

Environmental threats

To help give some perspective on what is sometimes a rather confusing picture, Table 1 lists some estimates of the major threats to the environment. No attempt has being made to put them in order of importance or comment on the accuracy of the estimates. That is still a matter of fierce argument.

It will be noticed that they are not all related to pollution. The extinction of species for example, is just as much due to the disruption of habitats – housing and road building in industrial countries, and deforestation in developing countries – as it is to poisonous wastes and herbicides.

The environment and opportunity cost

What has this varied group of problems got to do with economics? It will be argued, quite rightly, that they raise political, moral and social questions, as well as matters of scientific debate. Nevertheless, they all have one thing in common – **scarcity**. This is what economics is about – the arrangements that societies make for the use and development of their scarce resources. Environmental problems would not arise if there was a superabundance of resources. There would be no worries about running out of supplies. Most waste products could be easily and harmlessly dispersed if there were boundless oceans and atmosphere. Many of our environmental problems occur simply because we have tended to treat world resources as if they were limitless.

Scarcity forces upon us the necessity of making choices by comparing alternatives. If limited resources are fully employed, an increase in the output of one commodity or service can only be achieved by having

5

Table 1 Environmental threats

Over-population
- Now estimated at 5.4 billion, it is increasing by 90 million every year (equivalent to the combined populations of the UK, Ireland, the Benelux countries and Denmark).
- Estimated to stabilize at between 11 and 15 billion by 2100, this is more than the planet can adequately support.
- 90 per cent of the growth is concentrated in countries least able to sustain it.
- It is estimated that half the world's population will within two decades be living in mega-cities – with substantial slums and squatter settlements in developing countries.

Species extinction
- Destruction of forests and other habitats is driving an estimated 100 species of plants and animals to extinction every week.
- The losses are particularly serious in the tropical forests, which cover only 7 per cent of the earth's surface but are a home to between 50 and 80 per cent of the planet's species.
- Genetic material being lost may contain means of fighting diseases or improving crops.
- In the UK each year about 1 per cent of the 5600 Sites of Special Scientific Interest suffer damage which may be irreversible.

Destruction of the resource base
Depletion of finite, non-renewable resources is still a matter of concern but attention is now on the threat to renewable resources:
- Deforestation – tropical forests shrink annually by an estimated 80 000 square miles (1 per cent) each year.
- This probably intensifies the greenhouse effect because tropical rainforests take in carbon dioxide and give out oxygen.
- Fisheries depletion – most experts are agreed that the limit to sustainable landing of wild fish has been exceeded. In more and more waters, too few fish have been left to maintain stocks.
- About 17 per cent of the world's soil is now considered degraded by overgrazing, unsustainable irrigation and other types of poor land management.

Waste
- The UK produces more than 130 million tons of industrial and household waste a year. Over 90 per cent goes in landfill. More than two million tons are dumped in the sea.
- As nations produce more waste, the world is running out of places to dispose of refuse safely.
- Organic wastes and fertilisers in high concentrations can affect water supplies and cause serious health hazards. Persistent toxic wastes – pesticides, lead, mercury, etc. – become ingested by animals and plants. They may remain in the food chain, eventually reaching a dangerous level on a worldwide scale.

Air pollution
- Local air pollution – smoke, carbon-monoxide from car exhausts and nitrogen oxide from industry – if concentrated, can cause lung and respiratory illnesses.
- Worldwide air pollution – industrial emissions, sulphur oxides and nitrogen oxides – react with water vapour to create acid rain, which is harmful to buildings, plants and animal life. At least 22 Scottish lochs are acidified.
- CFC (chloro-fluro-carbon) gases contribute to the depletion of the ozone layer which protects the air from injurious ultraviolet radiation. A 1 per cent decrease in the earth's ozone layer can cause a 3 per cent increase in skin cancer and a 1 per cent fall in the yield of certain crops. It is calculated that over Europe a 10 per cent reduction has occurred in the ozone layer in the past 10 years.

Global warming
- Carbon-monoxide and other 'greenhouse gases' contribute to the trapping of heat between the earth's surface and the atmosphere. Consequent higher sea levels may produce damaging climatic changes.

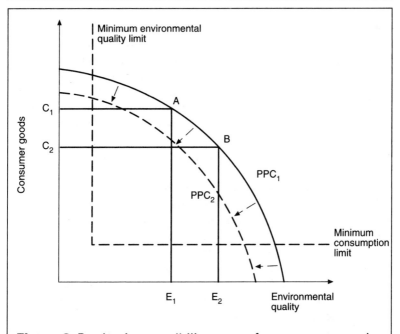

Figure 2 Production possibility curves for consumer goods and the environment

less of another – more resources used to clean up the environment means fewer resources available for consumer goods.

This is shown in a simplified form in Figure 2, with the production possibility curve (PPC). The curve PPC_1 shows, with given productive resources and technology, the choices facing a society. The vertical axis measures the amount of consumer goods produced, while the horizontal axis measures the alternative effects of using resources to raise environmental standards. This could be measured by an index of environmental quality including such things as air and water purity, toxic waste disposal and noise levels.

The curve shows the different combinations of consumer goods and environmental standards available. In practice it is unlikely that any community would reduce its environmental standards to zero – some minimum amount of waste disposal, for example, would be essential. Equally, no society, however 'green', will use all of its resources to raise environmental standards. The practical choices are indicated by the proportion of the curve contained in the dotted quadrant.

Assume that a society is at A on the PPC. The level of output is C_1 and environmental standards are E_1, and it is desired to raise standards to E_2. This involves the transfer of resources to environmental use and reduction of consumer goods output to C_2. This assumes, of course, that resources are fully employed and used efficiently. The tradeoff, the increase from E_1 to E_2 in exchange for a reduction of consumer good output from C_1 to C_2, is known as the **opportunity cost** of the increase in environmental standards.

Here it must be emphasized that decisions today about the amount of resources used for environmental standards may have an impact on the production possibilities for future generations.

Consider point A, with a high output of consumer goods and low environmental standards. In the long run this may reduce the PPC_1 to PPC_2 (dashed curve), as the productive capacity decreases with fewer healthy workers and less fertile land. With an eye on the wellbeing of future generations, it might be better to locate at point B, with a higher level of environmental standards. This may be a **sustainable output** of consumer goods, leaving enough resources for the environment so as to maintain the original PPC intact.

Whereas the PPC is, in the short run, a result of available resources and technology, *the position selected on the curve is a result of personal and collective choice*. Which point on the PPC is best? How much of its resources should the UK, or any other country, devote to the environment? The point chosen reflects nothing less than the whole range of alternatives, values, traditions and ways of looking at life which the society in question embraces. It is expressed through purchases in the marketplace and politically through the ballot box, lobbying and pressure groups.

Questions economists ask

The role of the economist is to help towards better choices by asking probing questions and providing, or encouraging the search for, relevant information on alternatives. Among the questions that economists ask are:

- What is the opportunity cost of achieving a particular environmental change?
- Is the environmental objective – for example, reducing output of CO_2, a greenhouse gas – being achieved in the most **cost-effective** way? That is to say, as cheaply as possible. Failure to be cost-effective means that the community is operating inefficiently at some point inside its PPC.

Environmentalism runs riot

SO EFFECTIVELY have environmentalists greened public opinion that it takes an unashamed reactionary to question the wisdom of becoming ever greener and cleaner. Most environmental pressure-groups are convinced that the environment is so important that standards cannot be set too high, and must be met regardless of cost. When an annual public-opinion poll asks Americans whether they share that view, a large majority agrees. Europeans, too, now tend to believe that anything greener must be better. Such belief will gradually come to haunt greenery's advocates. For nothing – not even cleanliness – comes free; and the costs of environmental policies are likely to rise sharply over the rest of the century. *If the green enthusiasm generated over the past four years is to survive in public policy, the enthusiasts must learn the language of priorities, and of costs and benefits.*

Such zeal has been enshrined in laws borne in upon the wave of popular environmentalism. America amended its 1970 Clean Air Act; Britain passed a tough new Environmental Protection Act; the EC introduced directives on bathing water, rubbish, sewage and a host of other matters. All these new laws are now coming into effect. At the same time, popular greenery has swept into power a number of politicians who take their environmental responsibilities more seriously than most of their predecessors did.

The combined effect of lots of new laws and energetic green politicians is – quite rightly – to raise the costs of being dirty. In the United States, which spends more than any other country on the environment, the cost each year of cleaning up now runs at just over 2% of GNP – equivalent to some 40% of American defence spending. By the end of the century, that figure could well be over 2½%. In Germany, spending on pollution control is almost as high, relative to GDP, as in America. In most OECD countries for which there are adequate figures, such spending is on the rise. Green zeal tends to outstrip reason because the true size of the bill is often hidden from those who insist it be paid. Central governments do not need to sign the cheques for most of the spending needed to deliver higher environmental standards. The money comes from local government or – increasingly – from companies and consumers. When the EC sets standards for member states, or the federal government for American states, the effect is similar; to induce a devil-may-care sense that somebody else can be blamed for the bill. And when the burden falls on companies, politicians sniff a free lunch, and tuck in their bibs. Companies complain, of course: but then, they would, wouldn't they? For industry's past has not been a story of environmental virtue.

Government intervention is essential to make sure that polluters pay the true cost of their dirty deeds. But too much intervention, or the wrong sort, can easily distort the market in ways that do more harm than good. And the more governments succeed in curbing polluters, the more difficult their balancing act becomes. When air, water and soil are truly filthy – as they are in parts of many industrialising countries today, or were in parts of the developed world half a century ago – the gains to health and happiness from almost any environmental programme will exceed its economic costs. Once the most egregious pollution has been cleaned up – as it has been, by and large, in the rich countries – the iron law of diminishing returns starts to take hold.

Source: *The Economist*, 8 August 1992

- What are the most appropriate ways of encouraging cost-effective solutions?
- How do we value environmental improvements and how do we know whether the right balance has been struck between costs and benefits?
- How do we assess environmental decisions whose impact stretches into the future?

These are some of the themes of the rest of this book. Failure to raise and answer these questions can lead to an over-zealous 'green at any price' approach (see boxed item) which is wasteful and fails to help the environmental cause. Neither dogmatism, mysticism nor fluffy philosophies to save the whales are any substitute for the questions that arise from the inescapable scarcity of resources.

KEY WORDS

Greenpeace	Scarcity
Friends of the Earth	Opportunity cost
Green party	Sustainable output
Eco-system	Cost-effective

Reading list
The Common Inheritance: Part 1–The Government Approach, HMSO, 1990.

Essay topics
1. 'Everyone expects to be able to drive their cars and have endless supplies of pure water from their taps but equally they expect to walk in the countryside and enjoy wildlife. Everyone would like the reservoir or motorway to be built somewhere other than where they are' (J. Wales, *Investigating Social Issues*).
   (a) Explain the following economic terms: opportunity cost; externalities; Pareto optimality. [12 marks]
   (b) Apply these concepts to the welfare economics issues contained in the above statement. [13 marks]
   [University of Cambridge Local Examinations Syndicate 1994]
2. (a) Explain why it is possible to regard pollution as an economic problem. [7 marks]
   (b) What economic policies might the government use to reduce the

level of pollution? [9 marks] (c) Discuss whether it is possible, or desirable, to completely eliminate pollution. [9 marks]
[Welsh Joint Education Committee 1994]
3. Why is the existence of consumer choice important for the efficient operation of an economy? Under what conditions, if any, might the choices of individuals conflict with the interests of society?
[Oxford and Cambridge Schools Examination Board 1993]

Data Response Question 1

Market forces

The following task is based on a question set by the University of London Examinations and Assessment Council in 1994. Read the extract, which is adapted from an article by S. Brittan, 'The green power of market forces' published in the *Financial Times* on 4 May 1989. Then answer the questions.

Economics is concerned with the allocation of resources in the face of all opportunities, costs and risks. The market is a mechanism for transmitting dispersed information unknown to any one central planner or computer and providing individuals with incentives to act upon it.

There has been a long tradition of market-based thinking on the economics of the environment. The standard example of an externality is that of the smoking chimney which inflicts costs for which the polluter does not have to pay. *The main reason for externalities is not excessive, but inadequate, use of markets and prices.* The chimney owner is unrestrained because there is no price to pay for the harm inflicted by his smoke.

The original economic approach was to put *a tax on the owner of the chimney and other polluters.* The tax can be high enough to impose whatever standard of purification the legislature desires. There is also a case to be made for some combination of taxes for external costs – and subsidies for favourable spillovers. There are other related ideas, such as marketable 'pollution permits'. The more modern approach is to say that adverse externalities arise because property rights have been inadequately defined. It is because no-one owns large stretches of the sea that there is an incentive to over-fish.

The principle 'polluter pays' is an attempt to use the property rights approach. This is not always possible, especially where many people are involved and transaction costs are heavy. The most obvious example crying out for action is for a *congestion tax imposed on vehicles coming into busy urban areas.*

1. Explain the meaning of the phrase 'The main reason for these externalities is not excessive, but inadequate, use of markets and prices'. [4 marks]
2. Examine and illustrate with a diagram the impact of putting a *tax on the owner of the chimney and other polluters*. [6 marks]
3. What policy could a government employ to deal with a situation where it feels that the desirable level of pollution should be *zero*. [2 marks]
4. Analyse the economic effects on firms and households of a 'congestion tax imposed on vehicles coming into busy urban areas'. [5 marks]
5. Why does over-fishing occur when property rights are inadequately defined? [3 marks]

Chapter Two

Economic causes of environmental problems

'The closed Earth of the future requires economic principles which are somewhat different from the open Earth of the past'
Kenneth Boulding

Introduction
Since it is so harmful, how is it that we allow environmental damage to happen? Of course, some environmental disturbance is unavoidable. Even the most basic level of human existence – breathing, eating, defecating- has an impact on our surroundings. Almost every activity from farming to travel makes demands upon, and pollutes, the environment. *Zero rates of extraction and pollution are not an answer.* The solution lies, rather, in conducting our economies and ourselves so as to minimize this impact. The ways in which this might be done are discussed in the remainder of the book. In this and the following chapters we ask an essential preliminary question: how does *avoidable* environmental damage occur in the first place?

A new model of the economy
To help us answer this we need a relevant model of the economy. The conventional circular model (Figure 3), familiar to students of macroeconomics, shows *on the lower loop* the flow of output between producers and households; and *on the upper loop* the flow of inputs to producers.

Although this model is useful, it has a serious limitation. Even if international trade is included, it is still a *'closed'* model. It takes no account of the interaction between the economy and environment on which it depends. This is also shown in Figure 3, with environmental connections added below the circular flow model.

The environment, represented in the lower part of the diagram, performs three functions:

- it provides resources
- it offers amenities
- it absorbs waste.

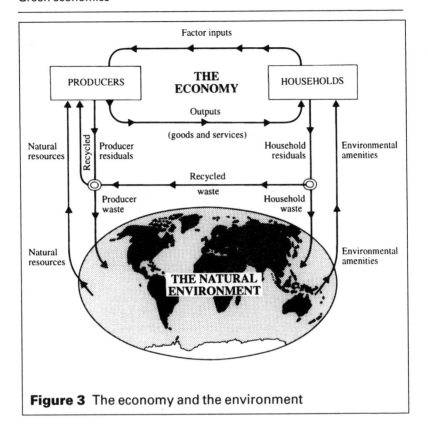

Figure 3 The economy and the environment

The flow of natural resources – minerals, water, energy, plant and animal life – from the environment to producers is shown on the extreme left of the diagram. This flow contributes in turn to the output of goods and services going to households. On the far right of the diagram we see, flowing directly to households, environmental amenities in the form of country walks, pleasant views and the opportunity for other recreational activities. Producers and households generate 'leftovers' or residuals, some of which are recycled to contribute once more to the flow of output. The remainder are dumped in the environment – labelled 'producer and household waste' in the diagram.

The three functions of the environment – as a provider of resources and of amenities and as an absorber of waste – interact with each other, sometimes in a competitive way and sometimes in a complementary way. Water is a good illustration of this.

The data in the boxed item show competing claims on water use in the UK. We can summarize the problem with a simple hypothetical

UK WATER DEMANDS

For manufacturing and processing

- One ton of aluminium requires 300 000 gallons.
- A four-door family car requires 100 000 gallons.
- One bag of coke requires 3000 gallons.

For households

- Two-thirds of the 3.8 billion gallons used daily in England and Wales is accounted for by domesic users. Domesic water consumption breaks down as follows:

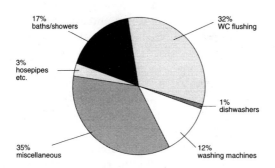

17%
baths/showers

32%
WC flushing

3%
hosepipes
etc.

1%
dishwashers

35%
miscellaneous

12%
washing machines

As a waste receiver

- 80 per cent by weight of all waste in England and Wales is liquid effluent dispersed partly to seas and estuaries but mainly to rivers
- 'The most important medium for receiving, processing and transporting liquid effluents' – Royal Commission on Environmental Pollution.

As an amenity

- 'The provision of amenity service is the third economic function of the environment. Thus in the UK the government has imposed a duty on the National Rivers Authority and the water companies to:

- 'conserve and enhance natural beauty and conserve flora, fauna and geological features of special interest'
- 'ensure that water and land are made available for recreation'.

Sources: Welsh Water plc; Water Services Association

example. The Rubicon River, as it flows into a populated area, provides water for industrial, agricultural and domestic services; this same water is discharged back into the Rubicon as effluent; and citizens of Rubiconia City like to spend their leisure time engaging in water sports and fishing. There is a limit to the capacity of the Rubicon to fulfil any one of these functions and it may be further reduced by its use for other purposes. Whether or not these uses are mutually exclusive will frequently depend on the level of use and the level of water in the river. High rates of effluent discharged, especially when the river level is low, would mean that for some purposes the water of the Rubicon could not be used as production input and it would certainly reduce its amenity services. When the river level is high, however, its ability to break down and absorb a given level of waste is increased and the diluted effluent is no longer a serious threat to other functions.

The spaceship economy

The new model helps us to see more clearly why things go wrong. In both our imaginary example and in reality, a river may become poisoned with waste; reduced to a sluggish trickle through excessive water use, or become so crowded with recreational users that it ceases to be enjoyable. Figure 3 shows why the river, or any other environmental resource, is misused. The vital links between the economy and the environment in the diagram are, for reasons explained in the following sections, somehow forgotten or overlooked, *so decisions taken in the economy about making the best use of resources pay little regard to the environment.*

Because the environmental links do not appear in market prices, in the balance sheets of producers, or in the calculations of national income, we tend to regard the environment as if it were a free resource. In an influential article 'The Coming Spaceship Earth', the American economist Kenneth Boulding claimed that many of our environmental problems arose because we tended to treat the world as a 'cowboy economy' with a limitless 'wild west' frontier of resources available for reckless exploitation. By contrast, as we come to realize our impact on the environment, we should think of our planet *'as a spaceship, without unlimited reservoirs of anything, either for extraction or for pollution'.*

Market failure

The great advantage of markets, when they are working properly, is that they ensure an efficient use of scarce resources. Markets generate

THERMODYNAMICS

Central to the view of the earth as a system with limited resources is the famous *First Law of Thermodynamics,* which states that energy and matter cannot be created or destroyed. In terms of our new model this implies that, if we wish to reduce the polluting mass of waste disposed of in the natural environment, the options open to us might be to:

- produce fewer goods and services
- reduce the amount of residuals generated in the production and use of goods and services
- increase recycling.

Energy cannot be destroyed, but the *Second Law of Thermodynamics* (entropy) tells us what happens – it is dissipated or transformed. The economy draws upon usable, low-entropy materials – minerals and fuel – from the environment. In turn, manufacturing and consumption generate less usable (sometimes useless) higher-entropy waste products, gases and wasted heat. This reminds us that, despite the scope for recycling, it can never be completely successful. Recycling itself uses energy and creates further waste. *100 per cent recycling is not economically feasible or socially desirable.*

There are three sets of economic reasons why in mixed economies (government sector plus private markets) we manage to ignore the lessons of thermodynamics and overlook the links between the economy and the environment:

- **market failure** (discussed in this chapter)
- **missing markets** (discussed in Chapter 3)
- **government failure** (discussed in Chapter 3).

information on scarcity, which is signalled in the form of prices. At the same time, prices provide powerful incentives to act on this information, as suppliers of capital and labour, in seeking to avoid losses and maximize income, try to make best use of their resources.

Nevertheless, the wasteful destruction of scarce environmental resources is an example of a **market failure**. Whenever a price becomes distorted or misleading, so that it does not provide a true signal of the underlying forces of supply and demand, then market failure occurs. Too much or too little is produced. The artificially high prices caused by monopolies are just one example. (See *Equity and Efficiency* by Margaret Wilkinson in this series.)

Here we are concerned with the impact on the environment of market failure caused by *externalities*. These are so named because they are costs (called **negative externalities**), or benefits (**positive externalities**), which extend beyond – and are therefore *external* to – the actions of a particular supplier or consumer. Thus the act of one household or firm imposes external costs or confers external benefits on another

---

DIRTY WASHING

The effect of smoke from a factory chimney was one of the earliest textbook cases of a negative externality. Quoted by the economist A.C. Pigou, in a pioneering study of externalities, *Economics of Welfare* published in 1920, it was based on an actual investigation in Manchester in 1914. This showed that households in the vicinity of the factory incurred costs of £290 000, caused by soot falling on washing hanging out to dry.

Today, in an era of washing machines, we would concentrate on studying the more injurious effects of emissions listed in Table 2. However, the principle which Pigou identified applies to all cases of pollution: the difference between **private costs** (in this case the cost of manufacturing and of inputs purchased by the factory) and **social costs** (the total cost to the community of the factory output). This should include the **external cost** of £290 000 for laundry bills. Because the laundry costs are external to the firm, they are not included in its bills or cost accounts – and therefore in the price it charges.

Private cost + external cost = social cost.

Remember that the so-called private costs must be included because the resources the factory output absorbs are not available to the wider community for any alternative use.

Table 2 Examples of environmental externalities

	Negative (cost)	Positive (benefit)
Consumer to consumer	• Car exhaust fumes/noise • Traffic congestion • Street litter, especially from take-aways	• Well-kept gardens are a pleasure to passers-by and raise the value of adjacent properties
Producer to producer	• A crop spray used on a potato farm which also kills insects that pollinate fruit trees in neighbouring orchards • Depletion of fish stocks	• A farmer improving land drainage may at the same time improve adjacent land on other farms
Producer to consumer	• Any waste or emission dumped or discharged in the environment without taking account of the external costs	• Any pleasant aroma from a coffee or chocolate factory, perfumery or bakery

household or firm. These external costs or benefits are not transmitted through prices.

Both positive and negative externalities can arise between producers, between consumers, or between producers and consumers.

Negative externalities

Figure 4 illustrates a negative externality. It might, for example, be the cost of acid rain, damaging to forestry and fishing, created by sulphur dioxide fumes from coal-fired power stations. The acid rain damage is shown as MEC, the marginal external cost curve – the damage caused by an extra unit of output. The curve is upward sloping, as for most types of pollution, because the forests and fisheries become worse at an increasing rate with continuing exposure to the pollutant. It is assumed that the power stations have a fixed technology and can only alter emissions by reducing output.

The supply curve, assuming a perfectly competitive industry, is S, which is derived from the horizontal sum of the marginal private cost curves (MPC) of the firms in the industry. The demand curve D is, at the same time, also a measure of how much the community is willing to pay for an extra unit of output from the power stations – the marginal social benefit (MSB = D). The competitive industry produces the output which maximizes profits, where supply is equal to demand –

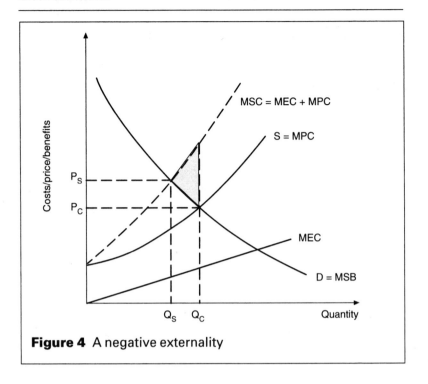

Figure 4 A negative externality

output Q_c at price P_c. From a social viewpoint, this price is too low and the output too high. It takes no account of the external costs. To do this we must add MEC to S (putting MEC on top of the S curve). We then get a full measure of marginal social costs – the MSC curve.

$$MSC = MEC + MPC.$$

The *efficient* output is at the point where the price P_s of the product is equal to the marginal social cost of production at output Q_s. This is efficient because at this point the extra cost of the extra or marginal unit of output, including environmental costs, is just equal to what the community thinks it is worth – its price, $P_s = MSC$. But the competitive industry produces an output Q_c at which point the price P_c is less than the MSC. This tells us that output is too high and too much sulphur dioxide is being discharged into the atmosphere.

The cost of the inefficiency is the shaded area – all units of output for which MSC exceeds MSB. This is a loss without any compensating gains, and represents the full costs associated with that part of the output between Q_s and Q_c for which the community is not prepared to pay. Nevertheless, it is inflicted on the community because the price P_c is too low – hiding the external cost. The efficient level of output is at Q_s at a price P_s.

Positive externalities

Figure 5 shows how the consequences of positive externalities may be a level of output which is too low, and takes the example of a home-owner's garden.

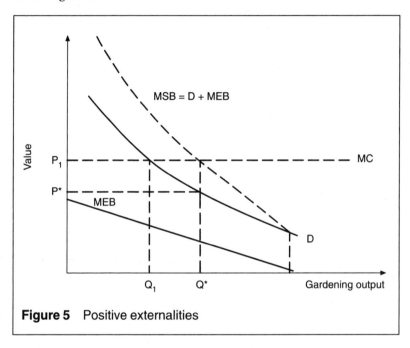

Figure 5   Positive externalities

The marginal cost curve for the investment of time and money in gardening is horizontal because the extra (or marginal) costs to the householder of planting an extra bed of flowers, it is assumed, will not be affected by the amount of gardening done. The pleasant garden generates external benefits to neighbours and passers-by, as the **marginal external benefit** curve (MEB) shows. This curve is likely to be downwards sloping in this case, because the marginal benefit may be large for small improvements to a very untidy garden, but less significant as further work is done.

The marginal social benefit (MSB) curve is calculated by adding the private benefit and the marginal external benefit together – putting the MEB curve on top of the demand curve D. Thus:

$$MSB = D + MEB.$$

The efficient level of output Q^* is at the point where the marginal social benefit to the community of an 'extra unit' of gardening improvements is equal to the marginal cost of the work. This is where the MC and MSB curves intersect. The inefficiency occurs because the home-owner does not manage to reap all the benefits from the investment in the garden improvements. Passers-by cannot be charged for the benefit they derive from pleasant gardens, nor then is there any way of reaping the gains from the impact on other property values. Consequently the price P_1 is too high to achieve the appropriate level of garden maintenance for the neighbourhood. The efficient price would be P^*, a pleasing thought for gardeners.

Suburban gardens may seem a trivial example, compared with world-wide environmental problems, but the principle established here has wider implications. *Wherever a positive externality occurs, not enough resources or effort will be directed towards producing the right amount of the good or activity which generates the positive externality.*

Remedies
How can market failure caused by externalities be remedied? This is discussed in more detail in Chapters 6 and 7. Here we briefly note two possibilities.

Regulations
Regulations could be imposed by the government restricting output to Q_s in Figure 4 – this is known as a **command and control system** (CAC).

A market incentive approach
This involves using the price signal to obtain the socially efficient output. This could be achieved by a tax on the polluting output (originally proposed by Pigou – hence the *Pigouvian tax*). If the tax raises the price from P_c to P_s, output is reduced to the desired level Q_s. The Pigouvian tax is a measure which is consistent with the **polluter pays principle** (PPP) – the idea that the price should include all external environmental costs. A sound idea this may be, but put into practice in the form advocated by its most enthusiastic supporters it could lead to some controversially high prices – for example, £138 for a hamburger (see boxed item). Read this now and *try the following questions when you have read Chapter 3:*

● How does this article illustrate both government and market failure?

Why a hamburger should cost $200

NANCY DUNNE

MOST economic modelling concludes that the arduous negotiating exercise recently concluded in Geneva under the General Agreement on Tariffs and Trade will give the world economy a new impetus.

Ecologists, however, believe the world's trade ministers can only tinker with an economic system that is fundamentally flawed by its failure to count the ecological costs of production. 'This could leave us with a world where there's lots of money but dirty air and water and environmental degradation,' says Alan Thein Durning, author of *Saving the Forests: What Will it Take?* from the Worldwatch Institute, an environmental group. What is needed is a system of 'full-cost pricing' that includes environmental costs in production of goods, he says. This would radically alter cost structures.

A mature forest tree in India would then be worth $50,000 (£34,000), according to the Centre for Science and Environment in New Delhi. A hamburger produced on pasture cleared from rain forests would cost $200. One hectare of a Malaysian forest, providing carbon storage services and helping to prevent climate change, would be worth more than $3,000 over the long term, according to Durning.

Environmentalists fear the costs of not moving towards ecological pricing will only become clear after it is too late. Deforestation is accelerating; two-thirds of the planet's original forests have already disappeared.

Political reform is also necessary to reforestation efforts. 'To varying degrees, a bond between timber money and political power is found in all the world's main timber economies,' says Durning. 'In less democratic societies, those who question the prerogatives of economic power all too often end up as murder statistics in human rights reports.'

Durning alleges that in countries like Malaysia – the world's largest exporter of tropical timber – elected leaders distribute to their loyal supporters contracts for the exploitation of public resources. Even in the US, the government moves reluctantly against the entrenched timber, mining and beef interests.

He would like full-cost pricing phased in over 10–20 years through user fees, green taxes and tariffs. He reckons that a $3-a-day charge to visitors to US national forests would raise more money than timber sales from US government-owned lands.

But first, governments must stop subsidising forest destruction. In the US the Clinton administration is edging towards raising prices for grazing lands, mining resources and, eventually, timber sales. Last April, it announced that it would halt the sale of timber from 62 of 156 national forests because of the money lost on timber sales. However, that decision has still to be implemented.

No country can move to full cost pricing alone without risking having their industries undercut by foreign producers whose governments do not make environmental destruction costly. Global action is necessary.

- What economic principle is being proposed here?
- What are the practical problems of such an idea?

Human action inevitably causes some environmental disturbance and damage. However, much of the environmental destruction that occurs is unnecessary and avoidable. It arises in part because of the failure of markets to provide the right price signals so as to minimize the environmentally harmful effects of pollution and consumption (negative externalities), or to encourage the good effects (positive externalities).

In addition to market failure we must consider the problems created by missing markets and government failure, which are discussed in the following chapter.

KEY WORDS

Market failure	Social cost
Missing markets	External cost
Government failure	Command/control system
Negative externality	Marginal external benefit
Positive externality	Pigouvian tax
Private cost	Polluter pays principle

Essay topics

1. Explain what is meant by market failure. Discuss, with examples, how environmental pollution may be reviewed as an example of market failure.
   [Northern Examinations and Assessment Board 1994]
2. (a) Explain what is meant by (i) private cost and (ii) social cost in the production of a service. [10 marks]
   (b) Discuss the extent to which it is possible and desirable to make private and social costs coincide. [15 marks]
   [University of Cambridge Local Examinations Syndicate 1993]
3. Examine the concept of opportunity cost in terms of (a) a decision to drill for oil in an area of outstanding natural beauty, and (b) a student's decision to continue in education after A levels. [50, 50 marks]
   [University of London Examinations and Assessment Council 1995]

Data Response Question 2

A market for waste paper

This task is based on a question set by the Oxford and Cambridge Schools Examination Board and University of Cambridge Local Examinations Syndicate in 1993. Read the extract, which is adapted from an article in the *Yorkshire Evening Post* on 1 February 1990. Then answer the questions.

A waste paper recycling scheme run by Leeds City Council which has raised thousands of pounds for charity could be forced to close – by the success of the 'green' revolution.

The price of waste paper has dropped by nearly 60 per cent since September of last year – from £12 to £5 per tonne. It costs the council an average ot £6 per tonne to run and administer the scheme.

That means the council's 'Save Waste and Prosper' (SWAP) scheme, which raised £20 000 for charity last year, is now having to pay £1 for every tonne it collects because the price of waste paper has dropped as a result of an increase in waste paper being recycled by environmentally conscious householders. There has been no change in the demand for waste paper from industry.

Some charity groups have abandoned their waste schemes because it is no longer worth their while to collect old newspapers.

SWAP chairman Liz Minkin admitted that the long-term future of the council's collection service was in jeopardy unless the Government introduced legislation to reduce the waste paper surplus. Councillor Minkin said the printing and newspaper industries should be forced to use more recycled paper in their products and that the market was in danger of collapse without regulation.

Operations Manager Peter Jackson said it would cost the authority about £17 per tonne to bury waste paper in waste disposal sites.

1. With reference to the information provided, use demand and supply diagrams to show how the market for waste paper changed from September 1989 to February 1990. [5 marks]
2. Economists identify three types of costs and benefits in the production of goods and services: private, external and social.
   (i) Distinguish between these three. (ii) Using the information provided as required, analyse the costs and benefits of the recycling scheme. [3, 6 marks]
3. Councillor Minkin believes that regulation is needed to encourage the printing and newspaper industries to use more recycled paper and so reduce the stocks of waste paper. What *other* policies might an economist recommend to achieve the same objectives? [6 marks]

Chapter Three
Efficient pollution, missing markets and government failure

'The phrase 'efficient pollution' enrages some greens and further convinces them that economists are completely insensitive to the environment.

The phrase **'efficient pollution'** appears to contain a contradiction because pollution is clearly harmful and it might seem absurd to imagine that it could also be efficient. Yet this is simply a statement about making best use of scarce resources. As Figure 4 on page 20 showed, even at the socially efficient level of output Q_s, some pollution from sulphur emissions will occur. This is not surprising since zero pollution would require no production, which might be quite unacceptable.

What is the efficient level of pollution? This can be seen more clearly from Figure 6(a) which just concentrates on the costs of the damage done by the pollution and the cost of reducing it (**abatement costs**). That includes the cost of pollution control equipment; the cost of inspection and the value of any output forgone in reducing emissions. The **marginal cost of abatement** (MCA) curve shows the extra cost of abatement arising from the reduction in pollution by one unit – measured here by the level of emissions. To understand the diagram, consider a movement from right to left – a reduction in pollution levels.

The steepness of the MCA curve will vary according to the type of pollutant. The MCA curve for reducing wastes discharged into a river, for example, will be different from that for lowering emissions of sulphur dioxide into the atmosphere. Nevertheless, the extra (or marginal) cost of extra reductions in pollution can be expected to rise as more valuable resources are drawn into further abatement. The marginal cost may become very high at low levels of pollution. Increasing the quality of river water from 85 to 95 per cent purity, it has been estimated, *may double abatement costs*. Similarly, totally litter-free streets, requiring a warden on every street corner, may be prohibitively expensive.

The **marginal social cost of pollution** (MSCP) curve measures the costs created by an increase in pollution of one unit – a movement to the right on the diagram. It is the same as the MEC curve of Figure 4,

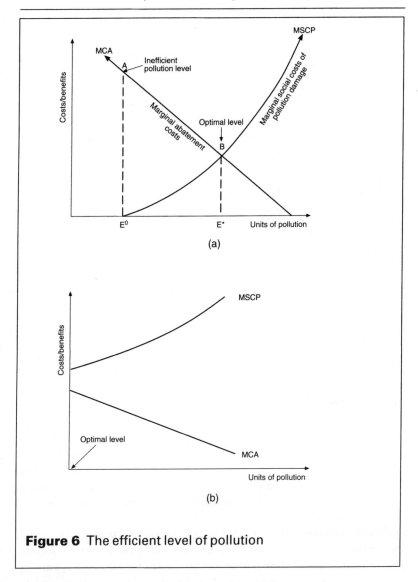

Figure 6 The efficient level of pollution

but relabelled to remind us that we are only talking about marginal social costs arising from pollution. The MSCP curve is sometimes zero up to a certain pollution level because of the capacity of the environment to absorb waste – by natural dispersion, by wind, water and biodegradation.

The efficient level of pollution is at E*, where the marginal social cost

27

of pollution is equal to the marginal social cost of abatement. If emissions were reduced further, to E_0, then the total abatement cost of reducing pollution from E^* to E_0 is represented by the area E^*E_0AB. The value of reducing the damage done by this pollution, and hence the value to the community for reducing it, is the area E^*E_0B. The costs of this reduction exceeds the benefit by E_0AB – a net loss for the community. *Any point to the left of E^* will be an inefficiently high level of pollution reduction since the marginal cost to the community will exceed the marginal benefit.*

The case of lethal pollutants, which are potentially threatening on a worldwide scale, such as plutonium or CFCs, is shown in Figure 6(b). Here the MSCP is above the abatement cost curve at every level of emission. *In this case the efficient level of pollution is zero, at zero output.*

Missing markets

How exactly do the problems associated with externalities arise? If each firm had to pay to emit fumes into the atmosphere, then socially efficient decisions would be made. But since no-one owns the atmosphere, there is no market and therefore no market price for clean air to guide businesses' and consumers' decisions. Firms have every incentive to pollute because clean air is mistakenly regarded as a *free good* with a price of zero.

Property rights

The connection between missing markets and the absence of property rights was first analysed by the Nobel Prize winning economist, Ronald Coase. If resources are not owned, they will be wasted because no price will be charged for their use. Coase argued that if property rights are well-defined, individuals will benefit by bargaining for use of the scarce resources – **Coase bargaining** as it is sometimes called – thus creating a market.

This internalizes the externality which is included in the market price and ensures an efficient outcome. A possible answer to environmental problems, it is claimed, would be to extend and clearly define property rights in all natural resources. The scope for this is examined in Chapter 7.

The problems created by the absence of property rights can be shown in the following example. If fishermen have unlimited access to waters which nobody owns (Figure 7), each trawler will catch fish at a rate of C_1 and where marginal private cost (MPC) is equal to demand – assuming perfect competition in the fishing industry. If competition and modern technology cause the total catch of fish to rise beyond the

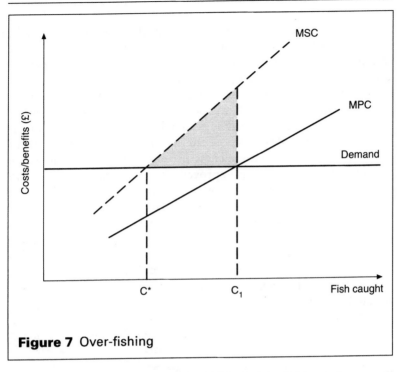

Figure 7 Over-fishing

natural replenishment level, stocks of fish and the fishing industry will eventually cease to exist. Although this is recognized, each individual firm feels that its catch is too small to make any difference. Competing trawlers will try to catch as many fish as possible while stocks last, so creating an externality by contributing to the extinction of the stock.

The marginal social cost curve (MSC), which includes the external costs of excessive fishing, indicates that the socially efficient level of catch would be C^*, where MSC equals demand. Individual trawlers, ignoring social cost, catch too many fish at C_1. The shaded area represents the social cost of over-fishing. If the property rights in the fishery were created and placed in the hands of a single owner, the problem might be solved. It is in the owner's interest to charge a fee to fishermen equal to the marginal social cost of fishing. This reduces the catch to C^*, which preserves stocks and the industry.

A practical problem arising from the solution suggested above is to exclude fishermen who don't pay. This might be feasible with the private ownership of a small river or lake, but impossible for the single owner of a vast resource such as an ocean. Some form of international cooperation with government regulation of the fishing industry may be necessary.

The difficulty of *exclusion* is common to what are known as **public goods**. This describes a type of good that may be supplied by private enterprise or the public sector, but usually the latter. With a **private good**, such as ice cream, people who don't pay can be *excluded*. Also, consumption is rival – one person's ice cream consumption means less for others. By contrast a public good, such as a lighthouse, is *non-rival* – an extra ship does not affect the availability of light for other ships. It is also *non-excludable* – no vessel can be denied the benefit of the light.

The quality of the environment is also a form of public good. If, for example, the purity of air is improved in an industrial area, everyone benefits because no-one can be excluded. But if we depended on the voluntary payments to secure clean air, people would be tempted to become **free-riders**, relying on the payments of others. Consequently, a private firm undertaking to purify the air will probably not earn enough revenue to cover the costs.

It follows from this that *private markets, if left entirely to themselves, are likely to under-supply environmental quality*. Although there is demand for, and a capacity to supply, environmental goods, the necessary markets are incomplete or missing. Some form of collective finance through taxation rather than individual voluntary payments may be necessary.

Congestion and public goods

When the use of a public good approaches capacity – a crowded national park or road network for example – it ceases to be non-rival. It becomes an 'impure' public good, with rival consumption, one of the features of a private good. Well below full capacity, an extra walker or motorist will have no effect on the consumption of other users. Also in terms of wear and tear, the marginal cost caused by extra use is virtually zero. Apart from the exclusion problem, this is often seen as a justification for not charging for public goods. Economic efficiency requires that marginal cost (zero in this case) equals price.

However, at peak times each extra walker or motorist, by adding to congestion, reduces the utility of others, so creating a marginal cost quite distinct from wear and tear. This is shown in Figure 8. At off-peak times, the marginal cost (MC) and average cost (AC) of travelling, measured in driving time, are equal. Beyond traffic volume V_1, congestion increases, as each extra driver inflicts a time delay on others. Since average cost (journey time) is rising, marginal cost is higher than average cost. The efficient volume of traffic is V_2, where peak demand (marginal social benefit) is equal to marginal cost; that is, MSB = MC.

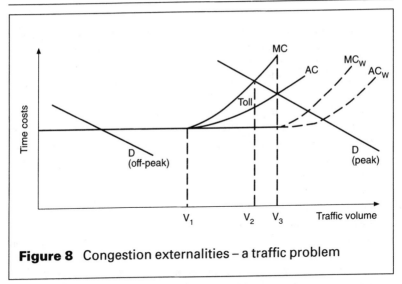

Figure 8 Congestion externalities – a traffic problem

Because this marginal cost, known as a **congestion externality**, is borne by other motorists, each driver is only interested in average journey time. Consequently demand increases to V_3 – an excessively congested and inefficient level of traffic, where marginal social cost exceeds marginal social benefit. A road widening scheme will reduce journey time but may create congestion externalities once again at an even higher volume of traffic as demand expands (dotted MC_W and AC_W in Figure 8). For example, the London orbital road (M25) was designed for about 80 thousand cars a day; but now its busiest section (in the south-west) carries up to 200 thousand a day.

This is another example of a missing market and missing market price, which is needed to internalize the congestion externality and bring marginal social cost into equality with marginal social benefit. A charge or toll for peak-period use could be the answer. This principle, subject to a satisfactory solution to the exclusion problem, can be applied to national parks, or any shared environmental resource where congestion externalities arise.

Government failure

So far we have identified environmental problems created by market failures. Can governments do any better? Disappointingly, government policies and activities, as a side-effect, can cause significant environmental damage:

- *In developed countries* there is sometimes conflict between environmental interests and government intervention to support fair prices.

The EU common agricultural policy, for example, intended to stabilize farm incomes and output, has increased the use of environmentally damaging pesticides and fertilisers. It has also encouraged the destruction of wildlife habitats such as small woodlands and hedgerows.

- *In developing countries* governments intervene with subsidies and controls – bringing prices below the market level – to assist the poor and promote economic development. These artificially low prices give the wrong signals, encouraging wasteful use of, for example, scarce energy and water resources. Although owned by governments, tropical rainforests are being destroyed, by concessions granted to commercial timber companies and peasant farmers, using the slash-and-burn method to clear land.
- *In command economies*, which replace markets by government controls, the record is even worse. The former Soviet Union, for example, now moving towards a market economy, is an environmentalist's nightmare. This is the legacy of the system which emphasized the achievement of planned output targets with little regard for consumers or the environment. Dissenting green views were suppressed. *Coase-style bargaining* between polluter and pollutees, to internalize environmental externalities, was unknown. Planners' targets ruled.

All of the problems noted above occur because governments fail to take account of the indirect environmental effects of their policies. Like market failures, government failures are also avoidable if corrective action is taken. This can be achieved by:

- ensuring that environmental standards are not overlooked by any government departments
- a systematic evaluation of all positive and negative externalities before starting any programme of government expenditure or legislation.

The latter provides a check on whether a proposed course of action is worthwhile – if the necessary social benefits exceed or are equal to social costs.

Summing up

The causes of environmental damage arise from a combination of related factors:

- externalities
- the lack of well-defined property rights
- the environment having characteristics of public goods.

These factors contribute to incomplete or missing markets. In turn these generate misleading prices, or no price at all, to guide producers and consumers towards socially efficient choices about the environment. To this list of causes we can add government failure.

However, many would assert that the major threat to the environment comes not from missing markets or from governments but from the pursuit of ever-increasing living standards or, less ambitiously, simply supporting an increasing world population. It is claimed that the higher output that this requires must involve the continuing destruction of natural resources. *Can we have economic growth and at the same time save the environment?* That is the theme of the next chapter.

KEY WORDS

Efficient pollution
Abatement cost
Marginal cost of abatement
Marginal social cost of
   pollution
Coase bargaining

Public goods
Private goods
Free-riders
Impure public goods
Congestion externality

Reading list

Bamford, C., *UK Transport Economics*, Heinemann Educational, 1995.

Economics and Business Education Association, Unit 6 in *Core Economics*, Heinemann Educational, 1995.

Wilkinson, M., Chapters 5 and 6 in *Equity and Efficiency*, Heinemann Educational, 1993.

Essay topics

1. Examine the economic arguments for using charges, subsidies or direct controls to reduce urban traffic congestion.
   [University of Oxford Delegacy of Local Examinations 1991]
2. Atmospheric pollution is often described as a negative externality. Explain what is meant by this. To what extent is the reduction of pollution in the UK possible through the operations of the market?
   [Northern Examinations and Assessment Board 1993]
3. (a) Explain, with the aid of examples, the main characteristics of (i) public goods and (ii) merit goods. [5, 5 marks]
   (b) To what extent is it desirable that the government should provide (i) public goods and (ii) merit goods? [6, 9 marks]
   [Associated Examining Board 1994]

Data Response Question 3

A market value on nature

This task is based on a question set by the University of London Schools Examination Board in 1992. Read the extract, which is adapted from an article by R. Atkins, 'Putting a market value on nature' published in the *Financial Times* on 18 August 1989. Then answer the questions.

In 1989 Professor David Pearce published a government commissioned report which has been described as a mix between an environmental economist's reference book and a how-to-do-it guide for politicians.

If adopted in full the report suggests a wholesale shake-up of the tax system, planning regulations, the accountability of government departments and the presentation of national accounts. The report does not offer an overnight solution. Many of the ideas have not got beyond the textbooks.

Hardline supporters of free market forces will be disappointed. Professor Pearce says *'letting people pursue the profit motive quite regardless of what happens is likely to lead to disaster.'* He favours moving away from the traditional 'command and control' regulations whereby bureaucrats rule 'thou shall not do'. Instead, market mechanisms are used to match the price of goods, services or investment plans with the desire to protect the environment. He says, 'If you are going to surrender a little bit of the environment – *the environment at the margin,* as it were – to economic development, then at the very least you must be sure what you are giving up.'

One solution is a cost-benefit analysis – the application of economic techniques to measure all the gains and losses from a project or decision. Moral arguments are replaced by economic sums.

1. Examine the major costs and benefits involved in reducing the level of pollution. [6 marks]
2. (i) Comment on the proposition that 'letting people pursue the profit motive quite regardless of what happens is likely to lead to disaster'. [4 marks]
   (ii) How might 'hardline supporters of free market forces' justify their view of total non-intervention? [3 marks]
3. How could the market mechanism be used to control pollution? [4 marks]
4. What is meant by the phrase 'the environment at the margin'? [3 marks]

Chapter Four

Sustainable development

'... development that meets the needs of the present without compromising the ability of future generations to meet their own needs.' World Commission on Environment and Development, 1987 – the Bruntland Report

The issues

Can the output of goods and services be raised to match increasing demand without damaging the environment? The demand comes not only from rising world population, but also from rising expectations of higher living standards. Worldwide we see the challenge to traditional values – the expectation that people should be better off and better educated than their grandparents or parents.

The pursuit of higher living standards now may result in a permanent lowering of living standards in the future. As Chapters 1–3 have indicated, this might happen because:

- we exhaust the world's natural resources
- we exceed its capacity to act as a sink for waste.

What are the implications of this for growth of the gross natural product (GNP)? Some argue that, since it is productive activities and certain forms of consumption which contribute to pollution, growth in GNP should be reduced. Others even advocate a zero growth rate in GNP. Against this there is the view that zero growth is no solution, because we would have fewer resources to clean up the present environmental problems created by past growth. Its supporters claim that increasing the growth rate of GNP would actually contribute to the solution of environmental problems, instead of causing them.

The economists' response to this is that both the zero-growth and maximum-growth supporters miss the point – pollution may be the result of the *misallocation of resources* rather than growth itself. Whatever its growth rate, a community can be engaged in environmentally damaging production and consumption activities. As explained in the previous chapter, this can occur because of externalities and 'missing markets', together with the absence of well defined property rights in the environment. As a result, inputs are wasted and goods and services produced without regard for their true cost.

The origins of sustainable development

Instead of a sterile argument over growth rates, environmentalists now find it more useful to ask:

- What conditions are necessary for **sustainable development**?
- How can we manage growth so that it does not destroy the resources – natural assets and manufactured assets – on which it depends?

The idea of sustainable development, with its stress on environmental management or 'good husbandry', is not new. First introduced by the forestry industry almost a century ago, it re-emerged as a key issue in environmental economics in the 1980s, amid the growing concern about the degradation of natural resources. It was put firmly on the international agenda in 1987 by the influential United Nations' World Commission on Environment and Development, in its report *Our Common Future*. Popularly known as the Bruntland Report (after its chairperson, Mrs G.H. Bruntland, prime minister of Norway), it emphasized:

- meeting the essential needs of the world's poor – jobs, food, energy, water and sanitation
- unification of economics and ecology in decision-making at all levels
- the need to promote and improve the quality of development while conserving and enhancing the resource base
- effective citizen participation in decision-making
- ensuring a sustainable level of population
- an international system which fosters sustainable patterns of trade and development.

Key ingredients of 'sustainable development'

Defining sustainable development is not easy, because it is a debatable concept involving – as the list above indicates – ethical judgements regarding what is right and fair, about which people will disagree. Twenty-four definitions are listed in Pearce's *Blueprint for a Green Economy*. Perhaps the most widely accepted definition is the one used in the Bruntland Report quoted at the head of this chapter. Below we review the meanings behind the words in the quotation and the various ways in which it has been interpreted in the sustainable development debate:

Development

Whereas **growth** refers to any increase in real GDP, **development** means living standards – either:

- an increase in GNP or consumption per capita, or
- an improvement in the quality of life, not only in terms of personal consumption, but including measures of health, education, leisure, social life and the environment.

A less ambitious view of sustainable development is simply 'non-declining consumption' (or quality of life) per capita. In this case the increase in resources would match but not exceed population growth.

Needs
In contrast to the standard economic definition of demand – willingness and ability to buy at specified prices – the use of the word 'needs' implies an ethical view about essential community and individual requirements, which must in fairness be satisfied. The Bruntland Report distinguished between 'essential needs' and 'perceived needs', which it saw as being socially and culturally determined. It warned that the satisfaction of perceived needs today may well prevent future generations from satisfying their essential needs.

Present and future generations
The reference in the quotation to the needs of present and future generations is concerned with two aspect of fairness, or equity: **intra-generational equity** (within generations) and **inter-generational equity** (between generations).

The significance of *intra-generational equity* for environmental issues lies in the fact that it is the world's poor in the north as well as the south who suffer most from environmental degradation but who make the least demand on environmental resources. Furthermore, it is the poorest of the world who rely most heavily on such natural assets as fuel wood; on vegetation for human consumption; on clothing and shelter; on wild animals and fish for protein and their dung and bones for fertiliser; and on untreated water supplies. The more these resources are depleted and degraded, the more people in the Third World will come to depend on technological substitutes and the greater the responsibility of the developed world to make this technology possible.

Consider the following statistics:

- The USA has 5 per cent of the world's population. It uses 25 per cent of the world's energy and emits 22 per cent of all carbon dioxide.
- India has 16 per cent of the world's population. It uses 3 per cent of the world's energy and emits 3 per cent of all carbon dioxide.
- The USA produces 25 per cent of world GNP (at market exchange rates) whereas India produces 1 per cent.

The question of *inter-generational equity* arises because the present generation derives benefits from using the environment as a resource base and waste sink, but the costs of such use are passed on to future generations. The most obvious example today is the nuclear energy industry, which is creating radioactive waste that will be extremely hazardous for a thousand years without having developed a safe system for handling it.

There are two broad views about how this time-separation of costs and benefits can be dealt with.

- The first requires that future generations are protected only from catastrophe, into which category fall global warming and ozone depletion. There the responsibility would end, and the resource depletion, species distinction, etc., would be tolerated for the benefit of the present generation, whilst future generations would have to cope as best they could with whatever they inherited.

- The second, more demanding interpretation, requires that future generations are enabled to enjoy the same levels of environmental consumption as the present generation. However, there are difficulties involved in specifying exactly what should be inherited (the stock of assets).

The stock of assets

If the present generation is not to deprive future generations of resources to satisfy their needs, then it should pass on a stock of assets no smaller than the one it inherited. This stock, or portfolio, of assets comprises:

> natural capital (renewable and non-renewable)
> + manufactured capital
> + human capital (skills and knowledge).

The aim of keeping this stock of assets intact is to maintain a sustainable flow of income. It will not be sustainable in the long run if, in the short run, it is boosted by depreciating the stock – for example, failing to repair worn-out equipment or to replant trees.

Should the stock of assets passed on to future generations be identical to that which we inherit – a constant portfolio? Clearly the idea of constancy is irrelevant with non-renewable resources (minerals and fossil fuels), since depletion is a consequence of use. In this case, the issue becomes one of **substitutability** between natural and manufactured assets. For example, some would argue that the complete exhaustion of fossil fuels and their replacement by solar energy technology is consistent with sustainable development. Good environmental management would require that non-renewable resources are not depleted before replacement technologies are developed or alternative mineral/fuel deposits are located.

Does substitutability also apply to the *renewable* (plants and animals) part of the natural asset stock? Would it be possible – or desirable – to pass on to the next generation a stock of assets whose composition has been changed – substituting manufactured for natural assets – but whose productive capacity is the same as that of the stock of assets originally inherited? For example, are smaller forests admissible because there are adequate manufactured substitutes for timber – or is the extinction of a species of plant tolerable, if synthetic substitutes are available for its medicinal properties?

Conserving **bio-diversity** – the variety in all life forms – is also essential for the maintenance for a good-quality stock of natural assets. It is the destruction of habitats such as tropical forests, rather than over-exploitation, which is the main cause of the probable loss of one million species in the last 20 years, out of an estimated total of perhaps 30 million species. Maintaining bio-diversity is not without cost. It may be impossible to preserve all species and have development, but as the environmental economist Pearce has concluded:

> *'We should only degrade or deplete our natural capital stock – particularly resources that may be irreversibly lost – if the benefits of doing so are very large.'*

'Mind if I smoke?'

Such important decisions require **cost–benefit** analysis, which is the systematic comparison of all costs and benefits, including externalities, extending into the foreseeable future (see next chapter).

Attitudes

Lester Brown, head of the Worldwatch Institution and a significant contributor to the Bruntland Report, has argued that the transition to a sustainable society requires not just a change in the way we manage our resources, but also a change in attitudes from the 'me now' concern of conventional economics to the consideration of 'others now and later'. The changes needed can be seen by comparing the dominant values of a sustainable society with those of our more familiar unsustainable society.

Most environmental economists agree with Brown about the importance of changing attitudes, although there is less agreement about how this might be achieved and exactly which values should be adopted.

- On the one hand there is the view that free markets, with their emphasis on the satisfaction of individual wants, undermine support for the wider community values essential for a sustainable environment.
- The counter argument is that markets can be a powerful way of expressing and ensuring green values. 'Green consumerism' has been successful in persuading many manufacturers to adapt their products to match the demands of a growing environmentally aware population. The 'deep greens', however, would claim that consumer preferences – for example, for unleaded rather than leaded petrol – are irrelevant because there should be fewer cars on the roads. The aim should be to reduce rather than change personal consumption.

Whatever views are finally espoused, the shift in attitudes is likely to come about by a combination of information, education, green consumerism and government action. The role of green pressure groups will remain central in increasing public awareness.

British policy on sustainable development

In the UK the concept of sustainable development was popularized in 1989 by the publication of *Blueprint for a Green Economy* (the Pearce Report), which was originally prepared as advice for the Department of the Environment (see the boxed item).

Many of these views – although some critics would say not enough -

---

BASIC ARGUMENTS OF THE PEARCE REPORT

1. Sustainable development is a necessary condition for survival.

2. Sustainable development entails adjusting economic activity so as to sustain the world's life support capacity. This implies:
   (a) maintaining the integrity of natural and semi-natural eco-systems
   (b) ensuring that the harvesting of timber and fish stocks takes place at sustainable yields
   (c) ensuring that discharges of waste occur at rates that are within the assimulative capacity of receiving environments
   (d) exploiting non-renewable resources at rates constrained by the development of replacement technologies so that future productive capacity is not reduced by current resource depletion.

3. A necessary condition for sustainable development is the correction for these sources of market failure. For this to be achieved the environment must be valued and environmental values incorporated into decision-making structures.

4. For private producers and consumers this means that the set of prices they face in the marketplace must be adjusted for environmental effects.

5. In the public sector, environmental values must be incorporated into decision-making structures. This can be achieved in three ways:
   (a) by extending the use of cost–benefit analysis to all public investment decisions
   (b) by introducing environmental conservation constraints into public investment programmes
   (c) by constructing national accounts to ensure that natural resource losses and gains are incorporated into measures of gross domestic product (GDP).

Source: Bowers (Banc)

---

were reflected in the British government's first major statement on the environment, *This Common Inheritance* published in 1990. In this White Paper the government announced its acceptance of the concept of sustainable development which it interpreted as *'living on the earth's income rather than eroding its capital'*. By this, the government meant *'keeping the consumption of renewable natural resources within the limits of their replenishment and handing down to successive generations not only* [manufactured] *wealth but also natural wealth'*.

It is too early to say whether these arrangements will be effective in shaping policy and changing attitudes, or whether the process of consultation will remain little more than an exercise in public relations. Details of the cutting edge of the government's environmental policy are reviewed in Chapter 6.

International policy on sustainable development

The most significant event in the promotion of sustainable development was the United Nations' conference on Environment and Development – the 'Earth Summit' – held in Rio de Janeiro, Brazil, in 1992. At this meeting world leaders committed themselves to the principles of sustainable development when they agreed to *Agenda 21*, an environmental action plan for the next century. They also signed treaties on climate change and bio-diversity; agreed a statement of principles on forestry; and established a Sustainable Development Commission to develop and monitor progress on the implementation of Agenda 21 (see the boxed item).

It can be seen that the Rio declaration echoes many of the themes raised in the Bruntland and Pearce reports, but will these ringing declarations really make any difference? Critics have argued that the Earth Summit produced few binding agreements and only a modest financial

---

THE RIO DECLARATION

This declaration, about balancing the need to protect our environment with the need for development, is based on the following principles:

1. Sustainable development – because we are concerned about people's quality of life.
2. The sovereignty of states and their responsibility not to cause environmental damage beyond their frontiers.
3. The importance of development so as to meet the needs of present and future generations.
4. The importance of tackling poverty, one of the root causes of environmental degradation.
5. Reduction and elimination of unsustainable patterns of production and consumption.
6. Public participation in decision-making and access to information.
7. Preventative measures to protect the environment in the absence of full scientific certainty.
8. Application of the polluter pays principle by including environmental costs in the prices of goods and services.
9. Assessing the environmental impact of major projects.

---

commitment. In the short run the impact is likely to be small, but Rio has put the environment firmly on the agenda of international conference tables and set in motion some changes that will gather momentum. Two legally binding treaties have been implemented and more are likely to follow.

Concluding comment

At the core of the idea of sustainable development is the role of the present generation acting as a custodian for a stock of assets which is to be passed on to future generations. As Lester Brown has commented in his book *Building a Sustainable Society:*

> 'We have not inherited the Earth from our fathers, we are borrowing it from our children.'

To help us decide what to preserve and enhance, we need to develop ways of valuing natural assets – i.e. atmosphere, oceans – which are not normally priced in the marketplace. The Pearce Report has drawn attention to the necessity of an appropriate system of national accounts which shows depreciation of natural assets. These and other issues of environmental evaluation are considered in the next chapter.

KEY WORDS

Sustainable development	Inter-generational equity
Growth	Substitutability
Development	Bio-diversity
Intra-generational equity	Cost–benefit analysis

Reading list
The UK's Strategy for Sustainable Development, HMSO, 1994.

Essay topics
1. Discuss the view that the cost of economic growth outweighs the benefits.
   [Associated Examining Board 1991]
2. Explain whether or not you regard high growth as a desirable economic objective. Discuss the implications of growth for (a) Britain and Europe and (b) the less developed world.
   [Northern Examinations and Assessment Board 1991]

3. 'Economic growth should be curbed worldwide to reduce the impact of negative externalities on the world economy.'

'Economic growth is necessary to increase living standards in both developed and developing countries.'

Explain the meaning of each of these statements. Analyse the extent to which economic growth may increase or decrease economic welfare.

[University of London Examinations and Assessment Council 1993]

4. Explain what you understand by economic growth. Does economic growth always lead to a net benefit for an economy?

[University of Cambridge Local Examinations Syndicate, 1994]

Data Response Question 4

Cost–benefit analysis

This task is based on a question set by the University of London School Examinations Board in 1991. Read the extract, which is adapted from an article by R. Atkins, 'Putting a market value on nature' published in the *Financial Times* on 18 August 1989. Then answer the questions.

'Amalgamating figures for gross national product with environmental statistics must be given the highest priority', says Professor Pearce in a government sponsored report. It would give, he claims, 'a fairer indication of true progress, or sustainable development'. His report focuses on two possible economic mechanisms: first, *'polluter pays' taxes* working on the principle of matching social costs with market prices. A 'carbon tax', for example, would mean consumers paying a sum estimated to compensate for the damage their consumption does through global warming.

Second are 'marketable permits'. Here the Government sells a limited stock of exchangeable permissions to pollute. Companies finding it expensive to cut down on emissions would be able to buy permits from others who found the costs less prohibitive.

Opponents of the report suggest that the weakness of the plans lie in the high administrative costs. Valuing forests, monitoring schemes, regulating polluters and penalising offenders may need armies of bureaucrats and economists.

Professor Pearce, however, would be satisfied with a pragmatic approach to valuing the environment, using best estimates and recognising that *precision in economics is impossible*.

'It requires someone to sit down and do the fundamental equations. If you think about it, that is the sort of thing everybody should be doing when they make a decision like buying a house, car or whatever. How much is it going to cost? What are the benefits going to be?'

1. What is meant by 'polluter pays' taxes as the principle of matching social costs with market prices? [6 marks]
2. What problems does pollution cause for the interpretation of GNP data? [5 marks]
3. Explain why 'precision in economics is impossible'. [4 marks]
4. In the light of the passage, examine the concept of opportunity cost. [5 marks]

Chapter Five

How much for the environment?

'An economist is a person who knows the price of everything and the value of nothing.' Adapted from Oscar Wilde

This chapter looks at three related questions which must be faced, in order to decide on the correct amount of resources needed to save and improve the environment:

- How much are natural assets and environmental quality worth?
- How can the benefits and costs of environmental changes be compared?
- Can the environment be included in national and corporate accounts?

Valuing the environment

How can we put a value on, for example, clean air, quietness, beautiful countryside or the preservation of an endangered species? Clearly they are all 'valued' in various ways but are not priced because markets for them do not exist.

Conventional economics distinguishes between:

- **economic goods,** which are scarce in relation to demand and bear a price
- **free goods,** which command no price either because they are available in great abundance, or because private property rights are not established – they are common resources.

It is mistakenly thought that – as the quotation heading this chapter suggests – economists have a narrow view of life, being interested only in 'economic goods'. In fact, establishing ways of valuing environmental 'free goods' is an important concern of modern economics. The following section briefly reviews the scope and limitations of the various techniques currently in use.

Physical damage valuation

If the physical effects of pollution are measurable – for example, damage to health, crops or buildings due to air pollution – then the costs of these impacts and the value of avoiding them might be calculated. In the case of health these costs would include medical bills and value of output lost due to illness. Although useful, the technique has limitations. It ignores, in the case of health, the distress of illness and has an unacceptably restricted approach to the value of fitness and the quality of life. It is of no help in cases of environmental damage where the physical effects, such as loss of landscape or species, cannot be translated into costs using market prices.

Willingness to pay
An alternative to concentrating on the cost of damage is to find out how much people are willing to pay for environmental improvement or preservation. There are two ways of doing this:

1. Revealed preference
This is known as **revealed preference** because, even where markets for environmental goods do not exist, consumers may indirectly reveal how much they value them, through other actions or expenditures. For instance, demand curves for the enjoyment of the countryside might be constructed from the travel times and costs people incur to reach their destinations, which can be regarded as a price paid for access to the countryside.

The demand for clean air and quietness has been inferred from comparisons of the prices of similar houses in areas differing in noise levels or air pollution. On a house costing £50 000, for example, various studies estimate that in certain areas a 10 per cent increase in air sulphur pollution might lower the price by up to £600 and a one-decibel increase in traffic noise by £250.

2. Stated preference
Typically this group of techniques (**stated preference**) involves the use of carefully worded questionnaires to find out people's **willingness to pay** (WTP) for environmental improvement, or **willingness to accept** (WTA) compensation for an equivalent deterioration in the quality or quantity of environmental assets. Illustrations, models and videos may be used to help make the questionnaire more realistic.

In its most simple form a WTP question might ask: 'How much are you willing to contribute to save a public woodland near your home?' It might be expected that, for a particular environmental good, the value at which people are willing to buy (WTP) would be equal to the value at which they are willing to sell (WTA). Disconcertingly, WTA values are usually significantly higher. No single, totally persuasive explanation has been found. Among possible explanations is the difficulty of replacing environmental goods with other goods. Stereos and mountain bikes, for example, are probably inadequate substitutes for the loss of woodlands. Higher compensation is required for the environmental loss.

A feature of some stated-preference techniques is the use of experimental designs, to construct a series of hypothetical alternatives from which individuals are then asked to choose. Instead of the question 'How much are you willing to contribute to saving the Elephant?', respondents might be asked to rank, in order of preference, alternative wildlife programmes for a given cost, with different levels of preservation in the numbers of elephants, rhinos and mountain gorillas.

This technique can be extended to include manufactured as well as environmental assets. For example, in determining priorities for a development plan a local government council may have to consider:

- providing more industrial jobs
- preventing the loss of open land
- providing new housing
- conservation of wildlife
- promoting tourism in the area.

Data would be presented in the questionnaire, on the **opportunity cost** of, for example, extra houses or jobs in terms of the loss of open land or wildlife. Residents would then be asked to rank alternative development plans. This technique therefore provides information on peoples' marginal rates of substitution or tradeoff between different goods or qualities of goods. If monetary costs can be put on one of the goods in the survey, then WTP can be estimated.

'Hello! We can't be far from civilization'

An obvious difficulty is that all the stated-preference methods rely on answers to hypothetical questions and may be subject to certain biases because respondents are not making real transactions.

Total economic value (TEV)

People may be ready to pay for environmental assets they never experience directly. Contributions to saving the Panda, for example, or other threatened species, may come from people who never expect to see the creatures in the wild except in television programmes or photographs.

- **Use value** is what people are willing to pay to use the environment – for recreation; as a source of agricultural land and materials; as a receptacle for waste.
- **Option value** is the amount people are prepared to pay in order to preserve the option to use some environmental asset at a later date. Even if the option is not exercised, the possibility of doing so may be a source of satisfaction.
- **Existence value** is what people will pay for the satisfaction of knowing that a species or habitat exists, although they will never visit or use it. Preserving the environment for one's heirs and for future generations, as well as a belief in the 'sanctity of nature', are among the sources of existence value.

Total economic value
= use value + option value + existence value.

Cost–benefit analysis

Definition

The efficient use of resources in any undertaking, whether private or public, requires that all relevant costs and benefits be identified and measured. If the calculations reveal that the benefits exceed the costs, the project should proceed, but if costs exceed benefits then it should not. Where there are several projects under consideration all of which indicate net benefits, but which are all mutually exclusive, then the project offering the highest net benefits should be adopted.

Thus stated, cost–benefit analysis (CBA) appears to be simple common sense, and indeed its underlying approach is widely used by industrialists in the private sector. CBA as practised today was developed for the public sector by economists in an attempt to identify and measure the wider social costs and the benefits associated with public investment, particularly where market prices were non-existent or distorted in some way.

Procedure

In 1984, the Treasury issued guidelines to be adopted by government departments when undertaking cost–benefit studies of investment projects. These included the following:

> *Identify the direct costs and benefits of each option and the indirect costs and benefits experienced in other parts of the economy.*

This procedure seems relatively straightforward but requires a little explanation and elaboration.

A distinction is often drawn between direct (or 'primary') and indirect (or 'secondary') costs and benefits. With an irrigation dam, for example, the **direct costs** include the cost of construction and land used for the dam, while the **direct benefits** comprise the net value of extra crops produced on the irrigated land. Whereas these are *direct impacts* of the project, there may be **indirect costs and benefits** that are sometimes unexpected.

Secondary benefits in this example might include increased opportunities for recreation made possible by reduced flooding, while secondary costs might arise from damage to saltwater fishing and wildlife because of the impact of the dam on tidal marshlands. Most secondary effects are externalities – social costs or benefits. They must be measured using the techniques previously described – although, as we have noted, it may not always be possible to translate them into monetary estimates.

All projects have gainers and losers. If for any individual affected by a particular project the benefits outweigh the costs, then undertaking the project is said to be a move towards what economists call a **Pareto optimum** – some people gain and nobody loses. (See *Equity and Efficiency* in this series for a fuller discussion.) No-one would dispute the desirability of such a move on grounds of efficiency. But in practice the Pareto criterion is not very helpful because most worthwhile projects inevitably involve making some people worse off and other people better off. In our example of the dam project, the farmers would gain and the anglers lose. Sensibly, cost–benefit analysis does not apply the strict Pareto criterion but requires only that the *total* benefits of a project should exceed the *total* costs regardless of how the costs and benefits are distributed.

In principle, the gainers could be required to compensate the losers, but whether this is possible or desirable is not part of a cost–benefit analysis. Cost–benefit studies leave unanswered the important question of the *fairness* of the income distribution impacts of a project. Fairness cannot be resolved by economists; ultimately, in a democracy, it is resolved by the expression of public opinion through elected representatives and pressure groups. The item below about Oxleas Wood reproduced from the *Financial Times* illustrates the controversies surrounding the identification of costs and benefits. Read it and then attempt the questions that follow.

Government drops disputed Oxleas Wood road scheme

RICHARD TOMKINS

THE DEPARTMENT of Transport yesterday scrapped plans to build a new trunk road through Oxleas Wood in Greenwich, south-east London, giving environmentalists one of their greatest triumphs in recent years.

The controversial scheme would have severely damaged one of London's last ancient woodlands and had been the target of vigorous campaigning by conservationists and local residents.

It had also attracted the attention of the European Commission which earlier this year started proceedings against the UK government claiming it had failed to publish a proper environmental assessment of the project.

The aim of the scheme was to provide a link between the A2 London-Dover road and the A406 North Circular by building six miles of dual carriageway leading to a new bridge over the Thames, the East London River Crossing.

Mr John MacGregor, transport secretary, announced in answer to a written Commons question yesterday that he was dropping the £283m project because the section passing through Oxleas Wood failed to meet the environmental standards now applying to new road schemes.

He said the government still intended to build a link road across the Thames because the plan formed a key part of its strategy to regenerate the East Thames Corridor. But fresh proposals would now be put forward, incorporating a design competition for the bridge and possibly a role for private sector finance.

Mr MacGregor added that his decision was 'quite independent' of the EC proceedings because the government remained convinced that the environmental assessment directive did not apply to projects already initiated when the ruling came into force.

The main reason for the government's turnabout appears to have been an acknowledgement that it had virtually no public support from any quarter for its stance. The last straw came in May when the British Road Federation, a lobbying group which normally argues strenuously for more roadbuilding, allied itself with the campaign to stop the road through Oxleas Wood.

Friends of the Earth, the environmental pressure group, said 'We have been campaigning to save the wood for eight years, so we are delighted that the government seems to have faced up to common sense'. But it also warned against complacency: 'The fact that the government is still planning to build the bridge leaves an axe hanging over the wood.'

Questions on the Oxleas Wood scheme

1. Can you complete a list of costs and benefits?
2. How easy would it be to attach monetary values to each one?
3. Why do you think the British Road Federation has supported the campaign? (For an explanation of the EU Environmental Assessment Directiveve, rfer to the section on European policy in Chapter 8.)

National and corporate accounts

A precondition for the management of environmental resources is a comprehensive system of measuring the stock and use of such resources.

Conventional national accounts – most notably GNP statistics – are fairly reliable indicators of economic activity but are clearly inadequate for environmental accounting because they do not distinguish between economic 'goods' and economic 'bads'. For example, in 1992 the oil tanker *Braer* ran aground in the Shetlands causing widespread pollution, loss of wildlife and the destruction of habitat, and the consequent clean-up operation caused GNP to rise. This shows that such defensive expenditures render conventional national income statistics inappropriate as environmental indicators.

More importantly, these statistics do not measure depletion of natural resources. *The exploitation of North Sea oil and gas provides a good illustration of how the use of resources is presented as an increase in income rather than as an initial increase followed by a decrease in natural capital.*

Over the last forty years, according to estimates produced by the New Economic Foundation and the Stockholm Environment Institute, although GNP in the UK has increased substantially and consumer expenditure has nearly doubled, the costs of commuting, pollution and cumulative environmental damage have significantly offset gains in the quality of life associated with personal income (see Table 3).

Proposals to adjust GNP figures simply by subtracting pollution-prevention costs do not deal adequately with the problem. *It is necessary to measure the change in the quality and quantity of environmental goods.* There are two possibilities – physical indicators and monetary indicators.

Table 3 The cost of growth in the UK, 1950–90

Millions of 1985 pounds	1950	1990
Consumer expenditure	96 475	274 744
Cost of commuting	2 053	9 660
Cost of water pollution	3 563	3 331
Cost of air pollution	15 587	18 121
Cost of noise pollution	703	1 052
Cost of loss of farmland	538	1 533
Depletion of non-renewable resources	11 794	57 877
Long-term environmental damage	35 583	80 669
Per capita index of sustainable economic welfare	1 100	1 136
Gross national product (GNP)	137 970	360 548
Per capita GNP	2 719	6 280

Physical accounts, in order to be manageable, would have to be highly aggregated and would not, therefore, distinguish between the ecological value of, say, one acre of farmland and another. Nevertheless, Norway, France and Canada have begun to construct physical environmental indicators. These are a necessary first stage in the development of an environmentally adjusted set of national accounts which require valuation of the physical changes in the environment. This is a difficult task but the United Nations is developing guidelines for standard systems of green national accounts using monetary valuation.

There is, however, no agreed national or international system of measuring social performance in the audited accounts of firms and other corporate organizations. Thus the current state of environmental reporting by corporations remains principally voluntary. Surveys of financial reporting indicate that some of the larger corporations have significantly increased information on the environmental impact of their activities. For example ICI (Britain's largest manufacturing company), in the first audit of its environmental policies, included information on changes in its energy consumption and the amount of hazardous waste produced. Nevertheless, the audited reports of the majority of companies, not surprisingly, reveal nothing about the extent to which their activities pollute the environment. Despite pressures for improved standards of environmental reporting in company accounts, from international bodies such as the United Nations and the European Commission, most companies use green reporting purely as a marketing tool, including only the good news.

KEY WORDS

Economic goods	Use value
Free goods	Option value
Revealed preference	Existence value
Stated preference	Cost–benefit analysis
Willingness to pay	Direct costs and benefits
Willingness to accept	Indirect costs and benefits
Opportunity cost	Pareto optimum
Total economic value	

Essay topics

1. With the aid of examples, explain the terms 'private benefit' and 'social benefit'. Explain what you understand by 'cost–benefit analysis' and illustrate and discuss its uses as a means of resource allocation.
   [University of Cambridge Local Examinations Syndicate 1993]
2. 'The deterioration of the environment makes gross national income a defective guide to economic well-being'. Discuss.
   [University of Cambridge Local Examinations Syndicate 1991]
3. Distinguish between private costs and social costs using examples to illustrate your answer. Discuss the importance of the distinction for a government considering whether or not to help finance the construction of a new railway line.
   [Associated Examining Board 1993]

Data Response Question 5

Market distortion leading to pollution
This task is based on a question in a new-syllabus specimen paper from the University of Cambridge Local Examinations Syndicate. Read the article which features Allied Carbides plc, and then answer the questions.

Allied Carbides plc, which is located in Huddersfield, West Yorkshire, is a major producer of carbon black, an essential ingredient used in the manufacture of tyres and similar rubber products. The company has a 70% market share in the United Kingdom, the remaining 30% of manufacturers' needs being supplied from imports. Allied Carbides has expanded its operations in line with increased demand over the 42 years that it has been based on its present site. The company now employs 180 workers, mostly in the manufacture of carbon black. It is located in an industrial area of the town but as its manufacturing site has expanded then so it has become increasingly in conflict with residents of a nearby housing estate who have complained strongly about the detrimental effects that the company's operations are having upon the quality of their lives and upon the local environment.

According to economics theory, the firm is producing in a situation where the market mechanism has failed to achieve the best allocation of resources due to:

- the problem of externalities
- its monopoly power

These market distortions can be illustrated by the diagram below which is taken from a recent economics textbook (J. Sloman and M. Sutcliffe, *Economics Workbook,* Prentice Hall, 1991).

There is no easy solution to the problem faced by the residents on the one hand and Allied Carbides on the other hand. An interesting new approach, put forward by economists, focuses on the idea of 'pollution rights' details of which are outlined below in an extract from a recent article on this topic.

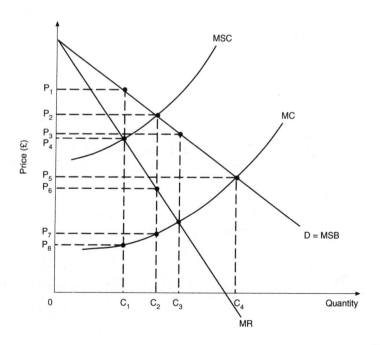

The traditional way of regulating pollution in the United Kingdom is by means of the *direct regulation* of industry, for instance by rules governing levels of pollution emission. The aim of measures such as the Clean Air Act and Alkaline Laws is to shift production methods towards those which make the optimum use of all resources, including environmental resources. Contrary to popular belief though, regulation does not eliminate pollution – it simply lays down minimum standards and as such, is unlikely to be as efficient as a *pollution charge or tax*. Taxation has various merits as a means of pollution control, although there are major practical difficulties to be overcome if so-called green taxes are to be accepted. In addition, it should be clearly stated that pollution taxes are relatively uncommon due to the political issues involved in their implementation. One particular concern is that the use of taxes in this way would be inflationary, although some would argue that this is a modest cost to pay for a more equitable and effective means of pollution control than direct regulation.

1. Why is Allied Carbides a monopolist? Analyse how you would expect it to operate relative to a firm in a more competitive market structure. [5 marks]
2. The following questions relate to the diagram:
   (i) What is the firm's profit-maximizing price and output? Explain your answer. [2 marks]
   (ii) What is the socially optimum price and output? Explain your answer. [2 marks]
   (iii) If a pollution tax were imposed equal to the marginal pollution cost, what would be the level of the tax rate? [1 mark]
   (iv) Given that the firm is a monopolist, what would be the new price and output resulting from the imposition of this pollution tax? [1 mark]
   (v) Would this be socially efficient? Explain your answer. [4 marks]
3. (i) Explain why 'taxation has various merits as a means of pollution control'. [7 marks]
   (ii) Why are pollution taxes inflationary? Discuss other likely economic drawbacks which might arise if pollution taxes were introduced in the United Kingdom. [8 marks]
4. The residents are pressing for Allied Carbides to relocate from their present site to one where they will be well away from people. Allied Carbides are not in favour of the move. As an economist, you have been asked to carry out a 'cost–benefit analysis' of this situation. Briefly describe the information you might need and how you could use it to arrive at an appropriate outcome. [20 marks]

Chapter Six

Environmental improvement in theory: government action

"The primary virtue of the price mechanism is that it signals to consumers what the cost of producing a particular product is, and to producers what consumers' relative valuations are. In a nutshell this is the elegance and virtue of free markets which economists have found so attractive since the time of Adam Smith.'
D. Pearce, *Blueprint for a Green Economy*, 1989

Preliminaries
We have seen how environmental damage can be caused when markets do not work properly or because the necessary markets are missing. This and the following chapter review the theory underlying the repair work that can be carried out using the economist's toolkit of ideas and techniques. Chapter 8 then looks at the environmental policies that governments manage to deliver in practice.

First we shall review two broad categories of alternative remedies – private actions and government actions.

- Private actions rely entirely on individuals and organizations, unaided by governments, to sort things out. Possibilities here include:

  - Coase bargaining (see Chapter 3)
  - **mergers** between polluter and pollutee to internalize an externality
  - **altruism:** increasing green awareness may prompt firms and consumers to produce and buy environmentally friendly products.

- When private actions are inadequate, government intervention may be necessary. This can be a mix of **command and control systems** and **economic incentive systems.**

Using command and control (CAC) systems the government sets pollution standards or limits. These are enforced by inspection and backed by fines and criminal prosecution for transgression. On the other hand, economic incentive (EI) systems use rather more carrot than stick, by providing financial incentives, often using price signals in market-based schemes. The following are some examples of EI systems:

- *Improving existing markets* with 'green' prices, corrected for the distorting effects of externalities by means of Pigouvian taxes or subsidies.
- *Creating new markets* by restricting the quantity of pollution, through the issue of a limited number of pollution permits that firms can trade between themselves. This internalizes the pollution externality by putting a price on it. Alternatively, congestion externalities (see Chapter 3), such as on motorways, can be internalized by pricing.
- *Market support,* in for example the encouragement of the recycling of waste, by means of packaging taxes, recycling credits and disposal charges.

Criteria

How do we decide which of these alternatives is the most effective? Taken from the influential book *Blueprint for a Green Economy,* the quotation which heads this chapter is enthusiastic about the virtues of markets, but in choosing between systems to combat environmental damage the following questions should be considered:

1. Cost

Is pollution being reduced in the most cost-effective manner? Does the anti-pollution strategy give incentives to find better and cheaper ways of achieving environmental quality? Environmental specialists describe this using the acronym **BATNEEC** – *best available technique not entailing excessive cost.*

2. Acceptability

Will the proposed solution command widespread acceptance in the community? This depends partly on whether it is regarded as equitable – not regressive in its income effects, and fair between polluter and pollutee.

The advantages and limitations of CAC and EI systems can be illustrated by comparing a 'green' or pollution tax with direct regulation in the form of an emission standard restricting the amount of pollution. Before we do this we need to make one more comment on variations.

Types of taxes and standards

In the example we shall consider below, it is the quantity of pollution which is taxed – an **emissions or effluent tax.** This is the most effective tax because it deals directly with the source of the damage. However, if the measurement of emissions is difficult or costly, then pollution may be taxed with an **input tax** placed on factors which contribute to the pollution – for example on unleaded petrol or fertilisers. Alternatively, outputs of the polluting manufacturer can be taxed – a **commodity** or **output tax.**

Instead of an emissions standard, the government may enforce a **technology standard,** insisting that firms use specific pollution-reducing equipment (e.g. gas filters on chemical refinery smoke stacks), or sell products that are designed to minimize pollution costs (e.g. cars with catalytic converters; aerosols without CFC propellants).

The impact of taxes and standards compared

In Figure 9, the socially efficient level of pollution is at 500 units, where the marginal social cost of pollution (MSCP) is equal to the marginal cost of abatement (MCA). An emissions tax of £2 per unit gives a powerful incentive for a firm to reduce its emissions to exactly 500 units, at which point MCA = £2. For any level of emissions above this it would be cheaper for the firm to reduce pollution to 500 units rather than to pay the tax because MCA is less than £2. For emissions reductions below 500 units the reverse is the case – the firm will pay an emissions tax of £1000 (500 × £2) and spend the amount indicated by the shaded area on clearing up pollution.

Compare this with an *emissions standard* of 500 units, vigorously enforced by inspection and fines, which appears to produce exactly the

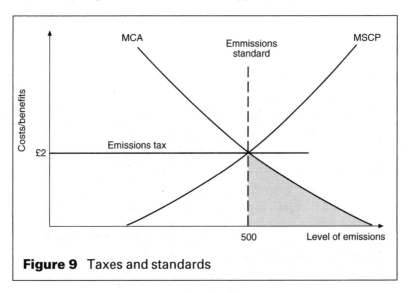

Figure 9 Taxes and standards

same socially efficient outcome. Is there nothing to choose between taxes and standards? Pollution taxes, it is claimed, are superior to standards in two respects.

Costs

Imagine two firms X and Y sufficiently close to each other for the environmental damage created by each firm's factory chimneys to be the same (see Figure 10). A reduction in emissions by firm X will therefore have the same effect as an identical quantity reduction by firm Y. However, because X and Y use different production equipment, the MCA curve of X is higher of that of Y. A daily total of 20 units of pollution is emitted – each firm's chimneys discharging 10 units. The government wishes to reduce the total daily emissions by 10 units and does this by restricting each firm's emissions by 5 units.

This is not the least costly solution. The total cost of abatement is equal to the area under the two curves between 5 and 10 units. It will be seen that this is inefficient because the marginal cost of abatement from 6 to 5 units is £6 for firm X and £3 for firm Y. Abatement costs would be lower if firm Y did more of the pollution reduction than firm X.

If an emissions tax of £4 is introduced in place of a standard, each firm will decide to what extent it is cheaper to reduce emissions and avoid the tax, or to pay the tax. Firm X, with the higher abatement

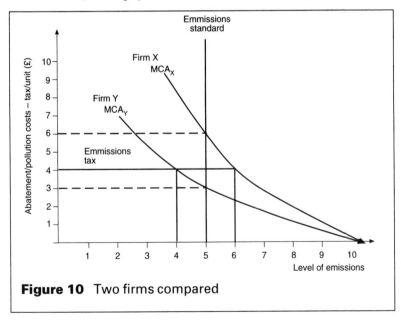

Figure 10 Two firms compared

costs, will reduce pollution from 10 to only 6 units but firm Y, with lower abatement costs, from 10 units to 4 units. At this point the marginal abatement costs of both firms are £4 – equal to the tax – conforming to the equi-marginal principle necessary for efficiency. With the emissions tax there is a saving in the total cost of abatement. The £6 marginal cost of abatement from 6 to 5 units for firm X, necessary with a standard, is replaced, under the tax, with a £4 marginal cost reduction by firm Y.

Incentives
With an emissions standard of 5 units, firm X has some incentive to adopt the superior technology of firm Y, moving to the lower MCA curve and reducing its costs by the shaded area. However, with the emissions tax the firm has an even greater incentive to reduce its abatement cost, because it will also reduce its tax liability. *Thus, tax provides a constant spur for firms to adopt the most efficient abatement technology and so achieve the cleanest possible environment.*

Does the polluter really pay?
A Pigouvian or pollution tax is popularly thought to be fair because it seems to force producers, who are mistakenly regarded as the only source of pollution, to pay the tax – the PPP principle. What about consumers? It can be argued that they must also share some of the burden because they buy the goods which ultimately cause the pollution. *In fact, the expense of a pollution tax is likely to be divided between producers and consumers.*

Faced with a tax, firms will probably attempt to protect their profits, by charging a higher price and trying to pass the tax on to consumers (see Figure 11(a)). Although after tax the price which consumers pay, P_t, is higher than the original price P_0, they do not pay the full amount of the tax. Some of this is paid by producers, who now receive P_t minus tax per unit sold – less than the original price P_0.

Figures 11(a)–(c) show that the division of the pollution tax paid by producers and consumers depends, *with a given supply curve*, on the *price elasticity of demand*. The less price-elastic the demand curve, the greater the proportion of tax paid by consumers – Figure 11(b). The more price-elastic the curve, the more will be paid by producers – Figure 11(a). The incidence of tax is shared equally in Figure 11(c).

Although there will be some welfare losses from the tax – producers and consumers will buy and sell less than before – the net effect will be a gain for the community. The excessive pollution damage, previously unchecked because of externalities, is now at a socially efficient level.

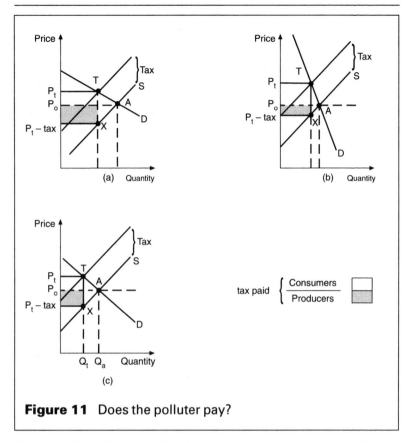

Figure 11 Does the polluter pay?

The tax-adjusted green price gives an accurate message to guide producers and consumers. If, for example, the demand for a good causing pollution is substantially price-elastic, then the green price will encourage consumers to switch to less damaging alternatives. The switch in demand from leaded to unleaded petrol, in response to a higher tax on the former, is a good example of this.

Pollution taxes are sometimes denounced because they seem to be harsh on poor people. The Institute of Fiscal Studies has, for example, calculated that a 15 per cent tax on domestic fuel in the UK would result in the poorest households having to pay more as a proportion of their income (1.8 per cent) than the richest households (0.1 per cent) – an example of a *regressive tax*. However, the regressive effects can be reduced by targeting income supplements and tax concessions to the less well off. Moreover, the revenues from a pollution tax can be used by the government for grants to firms to encourage the development of products and processes that are environmentally less damaging.

Why standards?

We have shown that use of a pollution tax – a market-based system - has in theory considerable advantages over direct regulation of the command and control (CAC) type. Despite this, CAC systems, especially standards, are still the most widely used means of pollution control for the following reasons.

Popularity

- Standards, which appear to promise to reduce pollution to definite levels, are favoured by politicians and the public. They are simple to understand and have emotional appeal. Even if standards are sometimes inefficient and not always enforced, headlines proclaiming 'tough anti-pollution legislation' are more likely to win votes than taxes. To declare something illegal gives the impression that action has been taken.
- Standards are popular with administrators because less information is required for the introduction of the standards than with taxes. They also gain, in preference to taxes, grudging support from industry, especially from large firms who see possibilities for **regulatory capture** – persuading the pollution regulators to be sympathetic and 'reasonable' when setting and enforcing standards.
- A strong reason for preferring standards is the difficulty in obtaining satisfactory international agreements between governments on terms of pollution taxes. If pollution tax is imposed by one country alone it may put its producers at a disadvantage compared with overseas competitors. However, it must be remembered that standards also create costs for an industry and international agreements on standards are equally desirable.

Safety thresholds

The vigorous enforcement of clearly defined standards may be the most suitable way of controlling highly concentrated, life-threatening pollutants – radioactive and certain chemical wastes – where it is essential that discharges are kept within tightly prescribed limits. In cases of this kind, safety rather than economy is clearly paramount. Nevertheless, for the bulk of pollution, the marginal damage curve rises only slowly. *In such circumstances market-based incentives, rather than standards, will produce a cleaner environment at lower cost.*

Markets in pollution rights

The advantages of market incentive systems can be combined with direct regulation by standards (refer back to Figure 10).

Assume, as before, two firms X and Y. The government sets an upper limit on total daily emissions of 10 units. Accordingly X and Y are issued with pollution permits allowing each of them 5 units of emissions. Since X and Y, without restriction, would each emit 10 units, a 5 unit per day abatement is required from each firm. The government allows the two firms to trade pollution permits between themselves for whatever price they can earn.

It will cost firm X, with the higher abatement curve, £6 to reduce its emissions from 6 units to the 5 units allowed by its permits. It would therefore gain, if instead of reducing its emissions to 5 units, it could buy an extra pollution permit for less than £6 allowing it to pollute up to 6 units. Firm Y, with a lower abatement cost, will find it profitable to reduce its pollution below 5 units, selling one of its pollution permits for more than £4 – its marginal cost of abatement from 5 to 4 units. Between £4 and £6, the pollution permits will be traded. Firm X will now emit 6 units and firm Y will emit 4 units.

Some critics mistakenly regard this exchange as unethical and call pollution permits *'cancer bonds'*. The market in pollution permits has simply internalized and priced an externality. Consequently, the target of a total of 10 units of pollution from X and Y has been achieved in the most cost-effective manner, in accordance with the equi-marginal principle. Firm Y, with lower abatement costs, makes the largest contribution reduction.

The creation of markets in pollution permits has been pioneered in the USA. In May 1992, for example, under the 1990 Clean Air Act, the Tennessee Valley Authority (TVA) bought an estimated £2.5 million worth of credits from Wisconsin Power and Light, which fell below its allowable limit of sulphur dioxide emissions. It is too early to evaluate the success or otherwise of these schemes, but the TVA transaction just quoted has been criticized for allowing further pollution in an already polluted area.

The success of markets in transferable permits will depend on many things, including: the initial allocation of permits; the competitiveness of the market; and the effectiveness of the agency running the scheme. However, such markets, properly organized, do offer the possibility of cost-effective ways of reducing pollution. They may also be more acceptable to industry than pollution taxes.

KEY WORDS	
Mergers	Input tax
Altruism	Output tax
Command and control systems	Emissions standard
Economic incentive systems	Technology standard
BATNEEC	Equi-marginal principle
Emission tax	Regulatory capture

Reading list
Anderton, A., Unit 5 in *The Student's Economy in Focus 1994/95*, Causeway Press, 1994.

Essay topics
1. 'As with all externalities, the proper way to treat them is to make those who cause environmental damage pay for it.' Discuss.
   [Oxford & Cambridge Schools Examination Board 1990]
2. Is atmospheric pollution an economic problem? What measures could the government take to alleviate such a problem?
   [Northern Examinations and Assessment Board, AS level, 1991]

Data Response Question 6

A market in 'permits to pollute'
This task is based on a question set by the Associated Examining Board in 1994. Read the following passage which is adapted from 'A market made out of muck' by Barbara Durr, published in the *Financial Times* on 10 June 1992.

The passage describes a scheme introduced in the USA which aims to reduce the pollution caused by coal-burning power stations. The scheme is based on setting, and then each year gradually reducing, maximum limits or ceilings for pollution. Under the scheme, a power station that 'over-complies' – that is, one that cuts pollution by more than is required – is allowed to sell its spare pollution allowances. The allowance or 'permit to pollute' can be bought by an 'under-complying' power station – one that has cut pollution by less than is required.

Note that 'one allowance' equals one tonne of sulphur dioxide.

Last month, three US utility companies bravely waded into a national experiment to use market principles for environmental ends and to tackle a problem of 'market failure'. In the first public deal to trade 'permits to pollute', the Wisconsin Power & Light Company sold 10 000 allowances to the Tennessee Valley Authority and between 15 000 to 25 000 allowances to the Duquesne Light Company in Pittsburg.

The allowances are part of the Clean Air Act of 1990, which requires America's mostly coal-burning utilities to halve their emissions of sulphur dioxide, the key ingredient in acid rain, by the year 2000. The national cap on sulphur dioxide emissions will be achieved in the most economically efficient way by trading the rights to pollute among utilities. Under the Act, those companies which exceed compliance with the emissions standard – by installing new cleaner technology or switching to lower sulphur fuels – can sell their spare allowances, issued by the Environmental Protection Agency (EPA), to those who have not fully complied.

The electricity market is a *'regulatory-driven market'*. As yet however, the public utility commissions that regulate the American private power companies have not spelled out who – the consumers of electricity or the companies' shareholders – are to benefit (or lose) from the effects on electricity prices and company costs of the trading of pollution allowances.

At present, surveys show that utility companies are tending towards over-compliance with the new standards – mostly by installing new technology to remove sulphur dioxide from flue gas, and some through fuel switching. The inclination to over-comply means that there will be extra allowances for sale. The price of allowances or 'permits to pollute' should therefore be kept pretty low.

In Phase 1, which runs from 1995 to the year 2000, 110 of the dirtiest plants have been targeted to reduce their emissions. Because most of these power stations are likely to install new technology to reduce emissions in preference to buying extra pollution allowances, the price of pollution permits will probably continue to remain low throughout Phase 1. But after the year 2000, in Phase 2, a permanent annual cap of 8.9m tonnes of sulphur dioxide will be applied to all the electricity generators. Assuming that demand for electricity increases, many power stations will find they are unable to meet demand while keeping within the pollution ceiling – solely by installing clean technology. To meet demand for power, they will have to purchase extra pollution allowances. In Phase 2 allowance prices are expected to rise to about $600 per tonne. This compares with $250–300 per tonne in the first deal. The EPA's penalty for emitting excess sulphur dioxide is $2000 per tonne.

1. Explain briefly why economists regard the formation of acid rain as a 'market failure'? [4 marks]
2. Explain: (i) the statement that the electricity market is a 'regulatory-driven market' and (ii) how consumers might benefit from the trading of pollution allowances. [3,3 marks]
3. With the aid of supply and demand analysis, explain why, according to the passage, the price of pollution permits or allowances is likely to rise from $250–300 per allowance in Phase 1 to about $600 in Phase 2. [6 marks]
4. The passage states that: 'The national cap on sulphur dioxide emissions will be achieved in the most economically efficient way by trading the rights to pollute...'.
(i) Briefly describe one other method, besides the creation of a market in pollution permits, by which sulphur dioxide pollution might be limited. [2 marks]
(ii) Discuss the advantages and disadvantages of the various methods of controlling sulphur dioxide pollution. [7 marks]

Chapter Seven

Environmental improvement in theory: private action

*'How, from shelves stacked with products labelled "non-toxic",
"recycled" and "natural", does the consumer know which to take
seriously?'*

This chapter looks at the highly pro-market view – *that private action,
not involving the government, can solve environmental problems.*

Coase bargaining, private property and mergers

We saw in Chapter 3, with the example of the over-exploitation of
fishing fields (Figure 7), how externalities can arise with a common
property resource, owned by nobody and to which everyone has
free access. As the economist Coase has pointed out, common property resources are likely to be misused and wasted. For instance, it
is said that the reason the Indian elephant survives is because it is
privately owned, whereas the African elephant, an endangered
species threatened by poachers – even in game reserves – is common
property.

The Coase argument (point 3 in the boxed summary) appears
to stand on its head the conventional wisdom that the polluter
pays. However, the polluter is not always rich and powerful and
the pollutee is not always poor and helpless. If polluters are
countries that are less well developed, or with inadequate technology
and resources, then financial inducements from the 'victim' are
essential. Examples of the victim paying the polluter can be seen in
the case of technical aid from Sweden to help Poland reduce its emissions of sulphur and nitrogen oxide that cause acid rain, and agreements to transfer technology to China and India to assist with
curbing CFC emissions.

Why, according to Coase, is the efficient outcome not affected by
who owns property? Imagine a factory whose operations require discharge of some waste into a river, which is also used by a firm running
a holiday camp with recreational bathing, boating and fishing.
Suppose an efficient solution requires the factory to install filtering
equipment to remove unsightly and toxic substances from the effluent,

---

THE COASE THEOREM SUMMARIZED

1. If property ownership is well defined, individuals well informed and bargaining costs not high, then the parties involved can bargain to their mutual benefit.

2. Externalities, positive or negative, will be internalized and included in the negotiated price, allowing a socially efficient output to be achieved.

3. Irrespective of who owns the property rights, a socially efficient outcome can be accomplished even if the pollutee pays the polluter not to pollute.

4. If bargaining is too expensive, it may be possible to seek compensation for pollution damage through the courts

---

making the river safer and more appealing to holiday-makers. The impact of the filtering plant on the factory and the holiday firm is shown in the first two columns of Table 4.

If the factory owned the river with the right to discharge waste, the holiday camp would gain if it paid the factory to install a filter. It might, for example, be prepared to pay up to £300 000 – half of its anticipated increase in the profit with a cleaner river – which more than compensates the factory for its fall in profits using the filter. Alternatively, if the holiday camp owned the river, with a right to clean water, then the factory would be compelled to install a filter if it wished to discharge waste. Regardless of property ownership, the same efficient outcome is achieved – filtered river water. The only difference that ownership makes is in the distribution of profits.

A merger of the two firms also solves the problem. Because the increase in total combined profit (the last column in the table) accrues

Table 4 Factory/amenity example

	Factory profits (£)	Holiday camp profits (£)	Merger (£)
No filtering equipment	900	200	1100
Filtering equipment	700	800	1500

Settlements pave way on pollution

ENVER SOLOMON

Two landmark out-of-court settlements yesterday opened the door for hundreds of people to claim compensation from official bodies for pollution damage.

In the first case a West Country beach owner who issued a £1 million writ against South West Water for sewage contamination won a clean-up operation.

In the second, the Harrods chairman, Mohamed Al Fayed, won compensation and costs from the Department of Transport and Surrey county council for damage caused to his estate by pollution from the M25.

Michael Saltmarsh, owner of one of the four private beaches in the country, took legal action against South West Water last August, alleging contamination from an outfall at Croyde Bay, north Devon.

Mr Saltmarsh, who bought the title to the Croyde Bay beach in 1988, would not comment on the financial details but said: 'I am delighted that I have achieved my main aim, which is to get the overflow drainage put right immediately.'

He said he had been considering closing part of the beach, which is used by up to 5,000 holidaymakers a day in summer.

His success is expected to pave the way for other claims. While local authorities would not be able to claim for profit loss, they could be asked for the, cost of beach cleaning.

Bill Foster, of the Marine Conservation Society, said: 'People will see this settlement as a signal that they should not accept poor conditions.'

A South West Water spokesman said the settlement terms included a number of measures to improve the sewage system at Croyde. 'Everybody wins – the environment and the people of Croyde.'

In the second case, Mr Al Fayed had sued the Department of Transport and Surrey county council last year over 'stinking' rainwater running off the motorway and seeping on to his Barrow Green Court estate, near Oxted, east Surrey. In the out-of-court settlement the department and the council agreed to pay him £5,000 in damages and nearly all his £250, 000 costs.

Mr Al Fayed said the pollution had ruined his 500-acre estate. He said the decision was a 'victory for the English countryside and everyone who wants a cleaner world.'

Experts expect the settlement to lead to hundreds of claims for compensation for pollution caused by motorways, possibly costing the Transport Department millions of pounds.

The Guardian, 16 April 1994

FRUIT AND HONEY

Fruit-growing and bee-keeping provide a good example of how Coase bargaining deals with, in this instance, positive externalities. Bees are essential to pollinate fruit blossom, which in turn provides the bees with nectar for honey. The positive externalities arise because extra fruit trees bring extra benefits to bee-keepers for which they do not have to pay. Also, extra beehives bring free benefits to fruit-growers. Theoretically we might expect an under-supply of orchards and bee-hives. However, because property rights in both are well defined, orchard-owners with trees low in nectar yield will pay bee-keepers to place hives in their orchards to achieve effective pollination. Conversely, bee-keepers will pay orchard-owners where there is high nectar-yielding blossom needed for honey.

to the merged company, there is a powerful incentive to install filtering plant. In this case, the diversification by merger internalizes the externality. The firm Ready Mixed Concrete, for example, diversified in this way into the leisure industry. The unsightly water-filled craters – an externality – left by its gravel digging were attractively landscaped and turned into a marina and theme park. However, mergers are usually undertaken to secure economies of scale and finance. They do not offer a general solution for externalities.

Implications and objections
For market enthusiasts, the Coase analysis appears to convey strong pro-market messages:

- If individual property rights are well defined, government action will not be needed. Private bargaining will deal with externalities.
- If common property resources are privatized and run for profit, by charging users for access, then most environmental problems would be solved.

However, can identify objections to the analysis.

1. Inefficient bargaining
Bargaining over externalities may be prohibitively difficult and expensive because thousands of polluters and pollutees are involved. With so many interested parties, **free-riders** are almost inevitable. Each individual has an incentive to leave others to do the work, but hope to reap

the benefit. Consequently insufficient effort goes into the bargaining.

Frequently information for efficient bargaining is lacking. This is a problem of **asymmetric information** – buyers and sellers have different information about a transaction. The exact sources of pollution may not be known. Moreover, one party may incorrectly believe that it can secure big advantages by tough bargaining. The factory in the example above might demand £600 000 and the negotiations would fail entirely.

In the real world, the ownership of property has a strong impact on bargaining outcomes. Farmers, for example, are a powerful and persuasive political lobby, influencing government legislation within which negotiations about externalities occur.

2. Privatization and externalities
Private ownership of property is clearly irrelevant in the case of a major source of externality – air pollution. It is also unlikely to deal adequately with over-fishing and ocean pollution. Quite apart from the trouble of satisfactorily dividing the world's oceans between countries and transferring ownership to private corporations, there remains the difficulty that fish will swim freely between seas; similarly with the movement of current-borne pollutants. Private ownership alone does not ensure the detection and policing, on an international scale, of the dumping and spillage of pollutants.

The failure of private ownership to deal with externalities arising from cross-boundary problems is also seen in agriculture. Toxic fertilisers used on one farm can percolate through the soil to underground aquifers, contaminating water supplies over a wide area. Likewise, new breeds of pesticide-resistant insects will move freely between farms.

Unless all externalities are internalized and appear in a firm's balance sheet, private ownership of resources provides an incomplete answer. Privatization of forests, for example, might save timber but will not save a single species of plant or animal if such preservation is not profitable. Even reforestation cannot be guaranteed if a logging company has a large enough acreage of timber to last over what it sees as its foreseeable lifetime.

The preservation of endangered species (see the boxed item) is a further example of how property rights do not get all relevant values on to a balance sheet and included in decisions on the best use of resources. Rhino and elephant farms may succeed in saving the animals, but is this the preferred solution? The 'for profit' answer is regarded by some as a distasteful variant of factory farming. Many people place a higher value on protection of wildlife in its *natural habitat*.

Altruism

If people are sufficiently unselfish (altruistic) and well informed, then in deciding between two almost identical products A and B they will buy B, the more expensive but less environmentally damaging product. In choosing B, consumers are internalizing the externality that exists with A. If there are enough buyers, profitable markets for green products will develop and many environmental problems will be solved.

Increasingly consumers have opportunities to buy environment-friendly products which sell at a premium. For example, they have a choice between free-range and battery eggs. There is no longer just 'timber' – there is wood from sustainable managed forests and wood of dubious origin (sometimes extracted illegally from indigenous native and biological reserves).

Assuming shoppers can afford green products, there remains the problem of asymmetric information. *How, from shelves stacked with products labelled 'non-toxic', 'recycled' and 'natural', does the consumer*

Rhino and elephant farms 'would save species'

DAVID NICHOLSON LORD

BIG animals such as rhinoceroses and elephants should be 'privatised' to save them from extinction, according to a leading South African wildlife researcher.

Rhinos, for example, should be farmed for their horn, which is widely prized for its medicinal and aesthetic properties and can be harvested without killing the animal.

International measures to curb trade in endangered species and conserve dwindling numbers appear to have failed, Michael Sas-Rolfes told a conference in London yesterday. Both elephant and rhino poaching continued despite millions of pounds spent by government and voluntary bodies.

Mr Sas-Rolfes is preparing a report on the rhino-horn trade for Traffic, a British-based body monitoring trade in endangered species and funded by the World Wide Fund for Nature and the IUCN (World Conservation Union).

He told the conference, organised by the right-wing Institute of Economic Affairs and described as the first in the United Kingdom to propose free-market solutions to environmental problems, that the 'mental block' of Westerners about the commercialisation of wild animals could propel many species into extinction.

He argued that the international ban on ivory has only affected Western countries, and demand for rhino horn remained 'substantial' and was unlikely to be reduced. 'As long as there is some demand, rhinos will continue to be under pressure', he said.

The Independent, 17 April 1994

know which to take seriously? Which is greener – a product made of bio-degradable material or of recycled material? Competing claims to greenness may be confusing for consumers and difficult to evaluate (see the boxed item). Many products are virtuously claimed to be 'green' but how many really are? The label 'recyclable' may mean very little when there are inadequate facilities to salvage cans and wrappers. The 'Earth' beer – presented as a breakthrough in environmental products, with the

---

Green claims on timber 'mislead consumers'

SUSAN WATTS

CONSUMERS are being misled by deceptive 'green' labels on timber in do-it-yourself stores, the World Wide Fund for Nature said yesterday.

A three-year study of timber companies had revealed a confusing proliferation of self-appointed logos and certificates, the WWF said. The report, *Truth or Trickery? Timber labelling past and future*, sparked a row at its London launch as proponents of two rival schemes, both called 'Woodmark', produced plans to certify wood and wood products as coming from sustainable sources.

In a keynote address to the seminar the Prince of Wales gave strong endorsement to one of the schemes, drawn up over the past two years by the Soil Association, and organic farming group. He has asked the association to inspect and certify the Duchy of Cornwall's woodlands near Liskeard. This scheme, which has the WWF's support, will operate under the auspices of the Forest Stewardship Council, an international organisation set up to monitor claims on sustainably-produced timber.

The rival scheme, devised by the Forestry Industry's Committee of Great Britain, a trade body representing the British timber industry, was criticised by the Soil Association as hastily put together for the meeting by an industry fearful of losing its authority. This would certify wood that met British regulations enforced by the Forestry Commission.

However, one retailer said his customers had less confidence in schemes based on government standards than in those seen to be truly independent. A representative from B & Q accused the director-general of the Forestry Commission of missing an opportunity to promote British timber by refusing to commit to an independent certification scheme, allowing British wood to compete with imported timber carrying detailed information on its source.

□ *Truth or Trickery? Timber labelling past and future.* WWF, Panda House, Weyside Park, Godalming, Surrey GU17 IXR. Tel: 01483 426444.

The Independent, 18 March 1994

slogan 'Suntory thinking about the Earth' – offered nothing more revolutionary than a stay-on can opener.

In this setting it is easy to see how **Gresham's law** (bad drives out good) will start to operate. The consumer may not know if product A (more expensive) is genuinely environment-friendly, but suspect that the claims are simply 'marketing hype'. The good products will be undercut by the bad and it will become increasingly difficult to sell genuinely green commodities. Because of asymmetric information, market forces will not ensure a socially efficient outcome. A case can be made for some kind of regulatory body, assessing and validating the claims of eco-labels (see Chapter 8)

Summing up

- Economic analysis shows that government action to deal with environmental problems will usually be more successful if it harnesses market forces, instead of replacing them entirely by direct regulation (CAC). Nevertheless, for practical and political reasons, CAC systems remain widespread.
- Private action based on property rights (Coase bargaining) or altruism will generate, through market prices, strong but inadequate incentives for the best use of environmental resources.
- Market forces alone will not solve environmental problems. Government intervention is needed to support and guide private action towards a better environment.

KEY WORDS

Free-riders	Altruism
Asymmetric information	Gresham's law

Reading list

Anderton, A., Unit 5 in *The Student's Economy in Focus 1994/95*, Causeway Press, 1994.

Essay topics

1. (a) Explain what is meant by an externality.
   (b) Examine the impact of introducing any two of the following:
   (i) pollution taxes; (ii) legal maximum controls of pollution emissions; (iii) tradeable pollution licence permits.
   [University of London Examinations and Assessment Council 1994]

2. In what sense is pollution of British rivers and beaches an economic problem? Discuss what economic measures might be taken to deal with pollution in general and explain whether or not you regard it as desirable to try and eliminate it.

[Northern Examinations and Assessment Board 1991]

Data Response Question 7

The true cost of the car

This task is based on a question set by the University of London Examinations and Assessment Council in 1994. Read the passage below, which is from an article entitled 'The cost of the car' in *The Economist* on 27 April 1991, and then answer the questions.

The last few decades have seen an astonishing growth in road traffic almost everywhere. In Britain, for example, the average daily traffic per mile of road grew by 34 per cent between 1978 and 1988, and by 52 per cent on motorways.

Now governments and cities are starting to listen to economists, who have been telling them for years that the use of road space should not be a free gift to motorists. Of course, motorists in most countries pay taxes: on the purchase price of a car, on a licence to use it, and on petrol. But the first two taxes increase the cost of owning a care not of driving it. And they are often low compared with the true cost of using road space. Even petrol taxes make no distinction between where a car is used, which greatly affects the costs imposed on others.

If drivers paid the true costs of road use they might switch to less congested times, or make fewer journeys. In southern California the average number of passengers per journey is 1.1. If that rose even to 1.5, travel times would drop by nearly a quarter and pollution by around a fifth.

The bluntest way to encourage this would be to increase petrol tax.

1. What is meant by the statement that 'the first two taxes increase the cost of owning a car, not of driving it?' [3 marks]
2. Explain the meaning of the words 'the true costs of using road space', noting the difference between private and social costs. Illustrate your answer with a diagram. [6 marks]
3. Why is building more new roads not likely to be a long term solution to the problem of travel congestion? [3 marks]
4. Consider the economic effects of a government reducing the road fund licence fee and, at the same time, increasing the tax on petrol. [4 marks]
5. Examine measures, other than those referred to in question 4, which might increase the efficiency of road use. [4 marks]

Chapter Eight

Environmental improvement in practice

'The regulatory approach has served Britain and other countries well in the past and will continue to be the foundation of pollution control.'
This *Common Inheritance* – first report, September 1990

'Economic instruments are inherently more flexible and cost-effective ways of achieving environmental goals. The government believes that the time has now come to deploy them more fully.' This *Common Inheritance* – second report, October 1992

Inevitably, because of our membership of the European Union, much of the environmental legislation now affecting the UK originated in Brussels. However, there are some British initiatives worth noting.

The quotations heading this chapter are taken from an important government statement, *This Common Inheritance*. The **regulatory approach** and the use of **economic instruments** are entirely different – and some would say opposite – ways of dealing with environmental problems. In Chapter 6 they have been described as CAC (command and control) and EI (economic incentive) systems. In practice, the government uses a combination of the two systems in the following ways.

Integrated pollution control
The core of UK policy is contained in the **Environmental Protection Act 1990**, a key element of which was the establishment of **integrated pollution control**. IPC recognizes that all the various elements in the environment are inextricably linked. By considering the total impact of releases to the air, water and land, the aim is to ensure that no one element is protected at the expense of others. It is hoped that IPC will eventually be adopted throughout the European Union.

Regulation
Implementation of integrated pollution control is the joint responsibility of HM Inspectorate of Pollution (HMIP) and the National Rivers Authority (NRA). Local authorities have responsibility for checking

air pollution caused by smaller industries and for monitoring waste dumps on local sites. When legislation before Parliament becomes law, Scotland will have its own environmental agency. For England and Wales, the NRA, HMIP and local-authority staff will be combined into a single Environmental Protection Agency. It is hoped that this will strengthen integrated pollution control.

UK REGULATIONS

Ambitious and sprawling

The principle underpinning the rules is the cumbersomely named 'Batneec' or 'best available technique not entailing excessive cost'. The task of applying it falls to the pollution inspectorate.

Its director, Mr David Slater, has a modern taste for 'long-term dialogue with companies', and for 'cost-benefit' analysis. He argues that 'We're not in the business of putting business out of business'. Instead, he and his inspectors like to spend time discussing with individual companies how they can minimise waste.

While environmentalists are increasingly willing to contemplate cooperation with industry rather than confrontation, many have regarded the inspectorate's measures – the industry's mellowing response – with suspicion.

In particular, they accuse him of having 'gone soft' on polluting industries during the recession. While there are indications in parts of government policy that environmental aims have been sacrificed because of the fragility of economic recovery – environment department officials say privately that they regard the construction industry as out of bounds at present – the inspectorate denies that it has come under such pressure.

Some of that suspicion may seem inevitable, given the history of mistrust between the environmental movement and industry. But criticism of the regulation and the inspectorate is justified, some economists say.

Mr Dieter Helm, director of Oxera, the forecasting group, says 'the structure that we have now facilities 'regulatory capture' [an over-sympathetic attitude towards companies by their regulator] because the inspectorate has so much discretion with applying the rules, and so much of the judgement depends on examining individual sites'.

A second weakness, he argues, is that the rules are 'technology driven, and not subjected to a proper scrutiny of costs'. In his view, the 'Bat' element of the 'Batneec' rule has been applied more than the 'neec', which entails more difficult analysis.

For example, he argues, under present rules, coal burning power stations are urged to fit flue gas desulphurisation (FGD) to cut sulphur emissions, which have been linked to acid rain. It is true that FGD is the best available technique for power stations, he says, but if cost is taken into account, it would be cheaper to build gas-fired stations.

Financial Times, December 1993

All firms with processes likely to pollute must first obtain authorization from HMIP, which can set specific conditions that operators must meet – for example, requiring them to minimize emissions or to make emissions harmless. An authorization is supposed to be granted only if the firm deals with pollution using the *best available techniques not entailing excessive cost* (**BATNEEC**). A record of all applications from firms and organizations is available for public scrutiny.

Under the Environmental Protection Act, directors and managers can be personally liable for their company's pollution. In theory, although so far never in practice, criminal charges can be brought against them and they can be sent to jail. The HMIP and NRA are considered to be the most vigorous pollution control bodies in Europe. On the face of it the UK appears to have a tough but fair regulatory (or CAC) regime. Nevertheless, there are doubts about its efficiency and effectiveness (see the article from the *Financial Times*).

Economic instruments

The problems with CAC systems are acknowledged by the government. The publication of the second report *This Common Inheritance* in 1992 restored the principle of economic incentives to centre stage, with the statement that in future *'there will be a general presumption in favour of economic instruments'*. This was further underlined in the 1994 version of *This Common Inheritance*, which emphasized the government's commitment to deregulation in favour of market forces:

> *'...there is always a risk that regulation will impose unnecessary costs on industry.'*

The report summarized the advantages of economic incentives and gave examples of the government's use of them (see the boxed item).

Water

To the list of economic incentives should be added the effect of water privatization under the Water Act 1989. This has meant that the cost of investment needed for environmental improvements in cleaning up beaches and river waters is now reflected in water charges which have risen by a controversial 42 per cent above the rate of inflation.

Monitoring by the National Rivers Authority appears to show that people are beginning to get cleaner rivers and beaches, although green pressure groups dispute this.

Prior to privatization, government minsters were often defensive and sometimes evasive about the poor standard of water – but, fearful of

---

ECONOMIC INSTRUMENTS

Extracts from *This Common Inheritance*
Third report, 1994 (Cm 2597)

'Economic instruments work by putting a price on the use of the environment and include emission charges, product charges and tradeable permits. They have several major advantages when compared with direct regulation:

- cost-effectiveness
- innovation
- flexibility
- informational efficiency
- public revenues.'

'Existing instruments or fiscal measures which have environmental effects include:

- the tax differential between leaded and unleaded petrol, which has been very successful in stimulating sales of the latter
- recycling credits to reflect the saving in disposal costs which result from recycling domestic waste
- VAT on domestic fuel and power, which should encourage energy efficiency in the home and contribute towards achieving the UK's carbon dioxide target
- a commitment to raise fuel duty by at least 5 per cent a year in real terms, which should help to meet the UK's carbon dioxide target
- industrial rationalization arrangements under the Montreal Protocol, to allow firms to trade quotas to reduce the cost of phasing out CFC production.'

---

unpopularity, they were reluctant to raise prices. Now with no financial responsibility to the water companies, they can be more critical of water standards and charges.

There are strong incentives for environmental gain but much hinges on the effectiveness of the Regulator – the Office of Water Supply (OFWAT) – to ensure that cost increases are fully justified and the burden distributed fairly between consumers and shareholders. We are also dependent on the vigilance of the NRA in checking that higher quality water resources are being achieved. (See *Privatization and the Public Sector* by Bryan Hurl, in this series.)

Roads

Traffic congestion is another problem it is proposed to treat using economic incentives. The government made it clear in the Green Paper *Paying for Better Motorways* (1990) that motorway tolls will be used to reduce congestion externalities (see Chapter 3) as well as to help pay for new roads. It is intended that, along with the 5 per cent fuel duty, road pricing will assist in the reduction of greenhouse gases and other vehicle emissions.

But as numerous critics have emphasized, motorway pricing will only be effective as part of a coherent transport strategy, which is at present lacking. Investment in reliable public transport is needed if motorists are to be persuaded to switch from private cars. Moreover, experience shows that some new road building simply adds to congestion by encouraging more traffic. Recognizing this, the government in 1994 reviewed its £23 billion road-building programme, scrapping some of the proposed new motorways. Inner-city road pricing, which might yield substantial environmental gains, is hardly on the agenda because politicians fear the wrath of motorists. (See *UK Transport Economics* by Colin Bamford, in this series).

A mixture of instruments

In the UK, economic instruments are seldom used alone. They are usually supported by a mixture of statutory controls, information, government advice and persuasion. The 50 per cent reduction in air-borne lead, for example, achieved since 1983, is due as much to the enforcement of technical standards – cuts in toxic metals in petrol; new cars using lead-free fuel – as to the tax differential of unleaded petrol. A similar comment can be made about the anticipated effect on fuel saving resulting from VAT on domestic fuel and power. The

impact of this 'green tax' on fuel consumption will be increased by more stringent energy conservation requirements in building regulations. An Energy Savings Trust has also been established to encourage people to invest in better insulation and energy-efficient boilers. Grants for insulation and draft-proofing are available for low-income households.

It has been claimed that this package of measures will allow Britain to meet its obligations under the Rio treaty on global warming, ensuring that emissions of carbon dioxide are no higher than in 1990. Sceptics claim that the energy tax has more to do with reducing the government's budget deficit than commitments to global environmental problems. They argue that reductions in CO_2 emissions are a bonus. Green taxes certainly enable governments to claim necessities as virtues.

Although environmental taxes may in principle be a more efficient way to raise revenue than conventional taxes, that does not make them popular. This was clearly shown by the government's defeat in the vote in Parliament on the December 1994 budget, forcing it to abandon the proposed 1995 increase in VAT on fuel from 8 to 17.5 per cent. Since domestic and business energy consumption are a main source of CO_2 output, cancellation of the VAT rise makes it more difficult to achieve, through economic instruments, the planned reduction in greenhouse gases. This in turn puts more emphasis on the regulatory approach in reaching the targets to which Britain agreed when it signed the Convention on Climate Change in Rio in 1992.

Summary of UK policy

The list of economic instruments in the earlier boxed item is a short one. Despite the government's strong commitment to market forces, a CAC system predominates, for the reasons outlined here and in Chapter 6. The following comment in the 1990 version of *This Common Inheritance* remains true today:

> '*It is as yet rare to find a full market-based approach, in which prices reflect all environmental costs and benefits.*'

European Union policy

The European Union must have a role in environmental policy because its member states are neighbours. Since one country's pollution may affect others, cooperation on environmental issues is essential. *But if the producers in the European single market are to compete fairly, the environmental rules under which they operate must, as far as possible, be the same in each country.*

In 1973 the Community's *First Environmental Programme* was launched. Despite this impressive title, Community environmental policy developed in a piecemeal way for the next 13 years. In 1986 the Single European Act (SEA), which removed all remaining barriers to trade, gave fresh impetus to Community policy by consolidating previous environmental legislation. The SEA added a new Article (103R) which expressly recognizes the importance of the environment. This states that action in the Community relating to the environment shall have the following objectives:

- to preserve, protect and improve the quality of the environment
- to contribute towards protecting human health
- to ensure a prudent and rational utilization of natural resources.

The grand policy statements contained in the Article are converted into detailed actions through, among other instruments, **directives,** which under the Treaty of Rome are binding on member states. All directives, including environmental measures, are subject to the principle of **subsidiarity** – so, wherever it is considered more effective, the action necessary to achieve a target specified in a directive is left to each member state.

For example, the *Environmental Impact Assessment Directive,* introduced in 1988, gave force to the principles expressed in Article 103R by integrating ecological considerations into the planning and decision-making processes in all sectors. Under this Directive certain categories of projects, such as oil refineries, power stations, chemical installations and motorways, must be subjected to an **environmental impact assessment.** An EIA has to identify the effects of virtually every environmental aspect of a project but the way in which the assessment is conducted is up to individual countries. In the UK, for instance, when dealing with motorway projects, the Department of Transport has its own *Design Manual for Roads and Bridges* (see the boxed item). Although this does not guarantee that future roads will be beneficial and beautiful, it does at least force decision-makers to consider environmental issues which they might have otherwise overlooked.

The Community has agreed, since 1973, to over 400 measures to protect the environment, ranging from reducing acid rain pollutants to the conservation of wildlife. Many of these measures are being successfully implemented, while progress on others, such as the community-wide eco-labelling scheme for environmentally friendly products,

DoT DESIGN MANUAL FOR ROADS AND BRIDGES
Contents of volume II- Environmental assessment

General principles of environmental assessment
- The aims and objectives of environmental assessment and how its results are reported
- The scope of environmental assessment

Mitigation
- Altering the line of the road
- Lowering the road into a cutting
- Screening by planting, earth bunds or barriers
- Moving or creating a natural habitat

Environmental assessment techniques
- Air quality
- Cultural heritage
- Disruption due to construction
- Ecology and nature conservation
- Landscape effects
- Traffic noise and vibration
- Vehicle travellers
- Pedestrian, cylist, equestrian and community effects

EXTRACTS FROM THE 1994 GENERAL REPORT OF THE COMMISSION OF EUROPEAN COMMUNITIES

'... the Community granted financial support to 111 demonstration schemes and technical assistance projects in the field of environmental protection.'

'The Council adopted the Regulation of allowing voluntary participation by companies in the industrial sector in a Community Eco-management and Audit Scheme.'

'[The] Commission adopted a proposal for a Directive on integrated pollution prevention and control (IPC) with the objective of replacing the current sectoral approach by an integrated approach, allowing more effective pollution control and cutting the costs to industry.'

'... the Commission adopted the second report on the application of the Directive on the conservation of wild birds.'

'The Council adopted a decision on a mechanism for monitoring carbon dioxide and other greenhouse gas emissions in the Community.'

is disappointingly slow. If each member state is to be confident that its partners are living up to their obligations under EU law, then effective implementation and enforcement are vital. Free-riding must be discouraged. An EU network of Environment Enforcement Agencies (ECONET) has been established to help develop common approaches to implementation. In addition, the Commission (the executive arm of the EU) monitors progress and reports annually on the results (see the boxed item).

Current EU policy is revealed in the fifth Environmental Action Programme – Towards Sustainability – adopted in 1991. This sets out the objective of 'environmentally sustainable development' and identifies industry, transport, energy, agriculture and tourism as key policy areas. Four categories of instruments – compare with the UK – are proposed for the attainment of environmental objectives:

- legislation
- market-based instruments
- general supporting measures such as improved data, scientific research and more information and training
- financial support mechanisms.

Reflecting the concerns expressed at the Rio Summit, the Programme also covers global issues such as climate change, bio-diversity and depletion of the ozone layer.

KEY WORDS

Regulatory approach	Directives
Economic instruments	Subsidiarity
Environmental Protection Act	Environmental impact
Integrated pollution control	assessment
BATNEEC	

Reading list

Anderton, A., Unit 37 in *Economics,* 2nd edn, Causeway Press, 1995.

Economics and Business Education Association, Unit 13 in *Core Economics,* Heinemann Educational, 1995.

Maunder et al., *Economics Explained,* 3rd edn, Collins Educational, 1995.

Paisley, R., and Quillfeldt, J., Unit 30 in *Economics Investigated,* vol. 2, Collins Educational, 1992.

Essay topics

1. Explain why the emission of pollution by a firm into the atmosphere or into a river may be economically inefficient. Evaluate two ways of reducing any economic inefficiency caused by pollution. [Associated Examining Board 1990]
2. Assess the arguments for and against subsidizing public transport. [Associated Examining Board 1991]
3. Explain what is meant by private cost and social cost in the production of a good or service. Discuss the extent to which it is possible and desirable to make private and social costs coincide. [University of Cambridge Local Examinations Syndicate 1993]

Data Response Question 8

This task is based on a question set by the University of London Examinations and Assessment Council in 1993. Read the passage below, which is adapted from an article in *The Economist* on 27 January 1990, and then answer the questions.

How can the recent tradition of tax reform be continued? One answer: explore environmental taxes. Most taxes raise revenue, but do economic harm – by penalizing jobs, say, or profits. Green taxes raise money and do good, by making polluters pay costs they otherwise pass on to others. That is more efficient than allowing polluters to treat air, water and lovely views as though they were free. Taxes are also often more efficient than regulation.

The simplest green tax would be on road transport. Plenty of transport taxes already exist, so no new tax need be dreamt up; lots of costs – congestion, lead and many nasty gases – are inflicted by motorists on others; and road traffic will be a growing source of pollution. The transport department projects a doubling in the number of miles travelled by 2025. So even to restrict pollution to present levels would mean halving emissions per mile. On present trends, the reverse may happen: the 20 per cent rise in new car registrations between 1983 and 1988 has been entirely due to a rise in the number of cars with engines over 1 500cc. Bigger cars usually use more fuel.

There are various ways of applying green taxes to transport including using taxes to reduce fuel consumption.

One way would be to raise petrol duty. High petrol prices give motorists an incentive to drive fewer miles, and to increase their miles per gallon. The real price of petrol is low by historic standards. To raise prices to their peak of 1975 would need an increase in duty from 3p a gallon on 4-star to about 148p. Impossible? Britain's petrol duty would still be lower than Italy's.

The Institute of Fiscal Studies calculates that a 55p rise in duty would cut petrol consumption by nearly 8 per cent (more in the longer run, as people bought smaller cars). It would raise £1.8 billion in revenue directly, and indirectly another £300m. If changes in the commercial use of petrol mirrored those in the personal sector, revenue might be another £900m higher – a total of at least £3 billion.

Most of the tax increase would fall on the middle income and wealthy households – the poorest rarely own cars. But among car-owners, the poorest tenth would find a 55p rise in duty took 2 per cent of their gross incomes; the richest tenth would lose less than 0.7%.

Other EC countries have higher car taxes on big cars. That would encourage people to buy smaller cars. But would it cut fuel consumption? Not necessarily. Car duty has no effect on the cost of an extra mile driven. And, while most small cars use less fuel per mile than big ones, some don't.

1. Suggest *two* reasons why the real price of petrol has fallen since 1975. [4 marks]
2. Analyse the effects of a 55p rise in petrol duty on (i) government finances and (ii) income distribution. [4 marks]
3. Compare the effectiveness of using increased petrol duty and differential rates of vehicle excise duty ('car tax') as methods of cutting fuel consumption. [6 marks]
4. Using a diagram, explain how environmental taxes can be used to help reduce the problem of pollution. [6 marks]

Conclusion

'Think Globally; Act Locally' Bill McKibben, *The End of Nature*

Markets and the environment

This book has shown how many environmental problems are also economic problems because they concern the use of scarce resources. The 'economist' in ancient Greece – a title derived from the words *oikos* (house) and *nemo* (manage) – was really a steward or estate manager. Not surprisingly, the first texts on economics were really manuals on farming. It could be said that environmental economics takes us back to the origins of the subject – the effective management of natural resources.

If the world's resources are to be used efficiently, information is needed on which assets are comparatively abundant, or scarce, in relation to demand. This knowledge enables us to set priorities for efficient resource utilization – the conservation and sparing use of scarce natural resources; the fuller use of those that are more abundant. In theory this might be achieved by a rigorous system of state planning and control. As the experience of the former Soviet Union and other communist countries has shown, the bureaucracies such command economies create are cumbersome, expensive and inefficient. By contrast, competitive markets rapidly generate information about relative scarcity in the form of prices. At the same time these prices also provide powerful incentives – through income and the inducements of profit and loss – to act on that information and use scarce resources efficiently.

As microeconomic textbooks frequently remind us, the great advantage of competitive markets is that they are – unlike command economies – supposed to achieve this without the need for government regulation and a costly hierarchy of state planning committees. It is the absence of timely information and the lack of incentives to use resources efficiently that has been a fundamental weakness of command economies, contributing to their decline.

Although environmental performance of former communist countries is deplorable, the record of mixed-market economies is also extremely poor, despite the proclaimed virtues of competitive markets. As we explained in Chapter 2, markets appear to produce and deliver private consumer goods quite efficiently, but they often fail with shared public and environmental goods. The American economist J. K. Galbraith described this predicament as one of 'private affluence and public squalor'.

The correct price signals needed to guide producers and consumers in the proper use of environmental resources are either distorted or absent due to:

- externalities
- lack of well-defined property rights
- the environment having the features of public goods – especially the free-rider problem.

The misuse of the environment due to *market failure* is sometimes increased by *government failure*. We expect governments not just to avoid but also to remedy the environmental pitfalls of the market-place. Unfortunately governments frequently fail to take account of the indirect environmental effects of their own policies. In the UK a good example of this is provided by the 1994 report of the Royal Commission on Transport and the Environment, which pointed out that the transport system was

> *'... not sustainable, because it imposes environmental costs which are so great as to compromise the choices and the freedom of future genera-tions.'*

This comment, it will be noted, raises the issues of *sustainable growth* and *inter-generational equity* discussed in this book. By the year 2025 the projected increase in UK road traffic, on the basis of current policies, is expected to be between 86 and 145 per cent – possibly as high as 300 per cent in some rural areas. This is regarded as unsustainable because of the costs of externalities – pollution, noise and accidents. The inter-generational consequences may follow from irreversible changes in the environment and the loss of alternative public transport.

Among remedies for environmental problems outlined in this book (Chapters 4, 5 and 6) are:

Economic incentives
- improving existing markets with 'green' policies attained by environmental taxes
- creating new markets – congestion pricing and trade in pollution permits

Regulation
- pollution control enforced by *emissions standards,* or *technology standards* backed by inspection and fines

Green accounting and auditing

- cost–benefit analysis
- national and corporate accounts and audits – showing environmental impacts

The government action needed to deal with environmental problems will be more effective if it harnesses market forces – the first group of options above – *rather than entirely replacing them by direct regulation*. Nevertheless, environmental taxes remain unpopular and the second group of options predominates. An Automobile Association (AA) opinion poll in the UK, for example, showed that 55 per cent of motorists would 'vote against' politicians intending to introduce road pricing or increase other taxes on motoring.

Economics and saving the planet

Does economics provide solutions to the world's environmental threats? Is the economists' toolkit adequate for the task? Undoubtedly its remedies will help, but it must be remembered that important issues which have a great impact on the environment do not arise simply from market or government failure. Examples are the problems created by population growth and the question of who bears the burden of resolving environmental dilemmas.

The latter issue is about equity or fairness rather than efficiency, not solved by market prices. How much of a burden should be borne by current generations for the benefit of future generations? The question of 'who pays?' also arises in the debate over the conservation of tropical rainforests. Developing countries argue, quite understandably, that they should not be expected to forfeit the gains from the economic development of their natural resources simply for the benefit of richer nations.

How highly do we value the environment and how much of our resources are we prepared to put aside to preserve and develop it? The appealing slogan at the start of this chapter is too simplistic. Global action is just as important as putting bottles in the bottle-bank. The latter does not necessarily lead to the former. Nevertheless, McKibben is right in stressing the importance of attitudes and our commitment to environmental conservation. It is not the task of economics to solve problems associated with values and attitudes. However, it can help by contributing to a realistic debate about the alternatives that confront us in the management of natural resources and the future of our environment.

Index